A CLIMATE OF JUSTICE

Loving your neighbour in a warming world

Anyone who thinks that climate change is neither a justice issue nor a deeply Christian one, needs to understand what "love God and love your neighbor" really means. Pope's book captures both and cleverly weaves love, justice, God, and climate into a prophetic call for action.

The Rev. Canon Sally G. Bingham
President: The Regeneration Project www.interfaithpowerandlight.org

A CLIMATE OF JUSTICE

Loving your neighbour in a warming world

MICK POPE

a. Acorn
Press

Published by Acorn Press
An imprint of Bible Society Australia
ACN 148 058 306 | Charity licence 19 000 528
GPO Box 4161
Sydney NSW 2001
Australia
www.acornpress.net.au | www.biblesociety.org.au

ISBN 978-0-647-53335-2

First published by Morning Star Publishing in 2017, ISBN 978-0-648-16420-3

Mick Pope asserts his right under section 193 of the *Copyright Act 1968* (Cth) to be identified as the author of this work.

A catalogue record for this book is available from the National Library of Australia

Cover and text design and layout by John Healy

CONTENTS

CONTENTS

FOREWORD

Is justice just a good thing, or a necessary one?

Does justice matter in our gospel conversations, or is it a side topic belonging only in our discipleship conversations?

These two questions, and all of the consequent conversations, exploration and engagement, are at the center of my life's work. As founder of The Justice Conference, author, educator, and pastor, I've had the opportunity to raise God's heart for justice with Christians around the world. Only a decade or so ago, I found that any conversation about justice with my fellow evangelicals was more likely to raise suspicions than support. Today I find the tide has turned: now they are keen to join the forums around civil rights, creation care, slavery, and poverty.

Mick Pope is not one of the newcomers. He has persevered through decades of difficult dialogue. Gently, insistently, he offers this book as a guide to reshape the conversation to the deeper question: *How can we become just, as God is just?*

As the space for dialogue opens, there is great need for voices like Mick's, which speak through the authority of Scripture to the structural injustices of our world. This is the exploration of the gospel with its feet on the ground, whereby the pursuit of justice and righteousness is the putting right between not only ourselves and God, but also between ourselves and others, and between ourselves and God's creation. This goes beyond merely the *doing* of justice, to the *being* of justice and calls us into the good news concerning, and the ministry of, the reconciliation of all things.

Generous Creativity is a phrase I've been using to describe the result when human creativity crosses with a deep understanding of our call to be involved in the reconciliation of all things. A Generous Creativity that inspires our God given imagination to seek the good of others and creation, more than moralism or duty, is where justice should land. But a hope-filled and energetic conception of justice is a hard picture to paint. Far too often book length treatments on justice are more mired in the commands of God than a deep understanding of God Himself. They press down more on our shoulders than quicken our spirits.

Mick's book avoids the common pitfalls of reducing justice simply down to ethical commands, a sense of heavy responsibility, or a heroic cause reserved for privileged people of compassion. His language is fresh and the story he tells is concise and compelling. His mastery of scripture doesn't bog the book down, as often happens, but seasons and enlivens the experience of following along as he argues for a Christianity reflective of the life of Jesus. His writing is filled with the inquiring mind of a scientist, the heart of an evangelical, the calloused hands of the campaigner, and the quick tongue of the scholarly preacher. It is a joy to read.

I wish more people would write books like this because some stories need to be told again and again in new and compelling ways. If we are to sing new songs to God so that we are forced to deal with the messy particularities of our life and context, then certainly our justice pursuits, how God describes the kind of worship He desires, should be sung or told in new ways with fresh language and relevant illustrations.

Is justice just a good thing, or a necessary one? Does justice matter in our gospel conversations, or is it a side topic belonging only in our discipleship ones? Mick beautifully answers these central questions while inviting us into a fuller experience of our humanity and deeper engagement in the world.

Tim Keller once wrote, "God's grace makes us just." May this book, and the glimpse of God, His Kingdom, and our calling that it provides be a means of grace in your life. May this book, and your engagement with it, be a small part of the grace that makes us just.

Ken Wytsma, Justice Conference

Books like this, even short ones, don't happen by accident or without the involvement of many people. It is over two years since Claire Dawson and I wrote *A Climate of Hope* (ACOH). I always knew I wanted to keep writing, and *A Climate of Justice* (ACOJ) is a sequel in many ways, as we didn't discuss justice issues in depth. When I first had the idea to write ACOJ, I had a few chats with my old friend Ben Thurley when he was still with Micah. Ben and I go back to our uni days and had worked together before on various things for TEAR. His big question has helped shape this book. He asked, "What will it do for me?" meaning in his role at the head of an advocacy organisation. You'll see in each chapter how I examine what various organisations are doing in the justice space, and this book is dedicated to those who work tirelessly for justice.

Of course, the other key is timing. When I saw Jon Cornford's excellent *Coming Back to Earth*, I knew Morning Star would be worth approaching, but it took *The Justice Conference* to announce that the 2017 conference theme was *Love Thy Neighbour*, that I knew the time was right to start writing. Many thanks for Zara Vaccari and Paul Favel from TEAR/Justice Conference for getting behind the book, and Morning Star for agreeing to publish it.

There are many others to thank. When I told my wife, she reminded me of Jim Broadbent's character Charles Stanforth in *Indiana Jones and the Kingdom of the Crystal Skull* when he said of his wife "The look on her face was a combination of pride and panic." She encouraged me to get writing quickly since the deadline has been pretty short to make the conference.

Big thanks go out to people who read chapters. Ben Clark from TEAR read the whole thing and made some helpful comments; note Ben that I have used miniscule words to replace larger ones (a joke he'll get). Byron Smith of Common Grace was kind this time, as the number of changes I had to make was considerably less than *A Climate of Hope!*

Byron is a details guy. Thanks to Steve Bradbury (Eastern College), Kuki Rockham (EFICOR), and Daryl Crowden (World Vision) for their comments. Barb Deutschmann was able to share her wisdom from years working with TEAR's Dhumba program, and Brooke Prentis was extremely generous in giving me an hour of her time on the phone to help me decolonise my language when writing of the terrible injustices done to Aboriginal and Torres Strait Islander peoples.

Thanks also goes to people who wrote sections of the book for me: Ken Wytsma for his foreword, Ruth Valerio of TEARFund UK for writing the introduction, my mate Jarrod McKenna for his reflections on non-violence, Byron on Maules Creek protests, Jo Knight of TEAR on the important *Renew our World* campaign, and Andrew Starr of International Justice Mission.

Thanks also to everyone who has written a recommendation on the back of the book; it's always a good start that someone has read the book before it goes on sale. And of course to Amanda McKenna, who has definitely read the manuscript, dotting my Ts and cross my Is. Ah you know what I mean. Behind every author is an awesome editor. Many thanks also to John Healy for his wonderful cover design and hard work in dealing with my many emails to get the back cover just right.

And to you, my reader. Read carefully and prayerfully. I hope and pray you become as passionate about climate change as any other justice issue. It's time the church roused itself on this issue. It's now or never.

I acknowledge the traditional owners and custodians of the land on which I have been writing this book, the Wurundjeri people of the Kulin Nation, and pay my respect to their elders, past and present.

INTRODUCTION

Earlier this year I planted a papaya tree on the shamba (small farmstead, about 6 acres) of an amazing man called Daniel. Having been invited out by the Diocese of the Rift Valley to talk to their leadership team about environmental issues, I spent some time in Kilimatinde – a village in the Singida region of Tanzania, the poorest area in the country. One day I walked from Kilimatinde down into the Great Rift Valley, to where Daniel lives with his wife, Theresea, and his four year-old daughter, Daniella.

Daniel has lived on and worked his shamba for all his adult life but had just taken ownership of it a few months previously. It was already producing a variety of crops: as he walked me round I saw sweet potatoes; chillies; cashew, mango, papaya, moringa and boabab trees, and he rears pigs. But he has big plans to develop the land – in particular to increase his papaya production so he can sell them in the city.

In many ways it felt idyllic as we spent a special seven hours together, sitting in the shade of a large mango tree, drinking soda and having lunch, cooking cashew nuts and discussing politics and theology. Before (literally) climbing back up the escarpment, Daniel brought out his guitar and we sat together and sang worship songs (yes we sang Ten Thousand Reasons!), and listened as he sang his wife a love song that he had written for her. At the end of our day together, I planted a papaya tree, to help Daniel with his 160 new trees.

But as we walked around his land and listened to him talk, one frightening question loomed over me: when will it rain?

As idyllic as it sounds, his land is dying. The fruit on the papaya and mango trees are not growing properly. The cashew nuts aren't swelling as they should do. His piglets are skinny. And his field of chilli plants have all withered and died. The rains are late, and with each passing day the situation gets worse.

Daniel is amazingly enterprising and hard working. He has been building a well that will help with the water problem. Literally building it. By himself. One shovel at a time. He cut the big rocks himself, carried them by hand to the well and put them into the sides. He has been working on it for years and it still is not ready. But he needs it now because without it his crops will die and his family will have nothing to eat and live on.

What Daniel is facing is part of a much bigger problem because the whole area in the Rift Valley is in trouble. Partly this is because people have cut down the trees. They cut down the trees to make room to grow the food they need to survive, and to make charcoal to cook the food. As any basic knowledge of precipitation tells you, where there are trees there is rain. Cut down the trees and the land becomes desert. This is local climate change.

But it is also in trouble because of global climate change. Our CO_2-producing actions have changed the weather patterns of our world, and people like Daniel are suffering as a result. Having talked about climate change for years, I now saw what it looks like to a family who are being directly impacted by it, and it made me see again how climate change is the single biggest issue facing us today.

It is this issue that Mick Pope is calling us to take action on in this great little book that you hold in your hands. As he makes clear, we are called to love our neighbours, and those neighbours are people living thousands of miles away as well as those living literally next door. We cannot love our global neighbours unless we come to grips with the challenge that is climate change and take positive action, both in our own lives and in calling our political and business leaders to act.

Mick provides us with a clear Biblical foundation for why climate change is something that all of us as followers of Jesus should be engaged with. As subsequent chapters take us through some of the key issues that climate change is impacting on today, it becomes clear that this is not a fringe topic for a few weird green keenies: this is as central to our faith now as the slave trade was for Christians in my country and elsewhere two centuries ago. It is a moral issue that we cannot ignore.

At the end of my time with Daniel – as the sun reached a point where it was cool enough to make the two hour return climb – he gave me two gifts. The first was a few seeds of a tree that he simply called 'the timber tree' and he gave them to me so I could plant new trees at home. The second was two small pebbles. He had nothing else he could give.

The seeds I have planted in pots at home, and I have been watching them slowly growing throughout the year. The pebbles I have in a little dish on my desk at Tearfund. At Tearfund, our aim is to follow Jesus where the need is greatest. My work there is focused on motivating and equipping the Church around the world to bring about large-scale Christ-centred change on issues that affect the poorest and most marginalised. Again, we have recognised that we cannot do that without tackling climate change.

The pebbles in my office remind me of a world in trouble; of people suffering and struggling because of all our actions. It is a reminder of the processes of millennia that have shaped that pebble and of how I am a part of the same community of creation. And it is a call to each of us to do as much as we can – however big or small – to create a different and better future.

Dr Ruth Valerio
Global Advocacy and Influencing Director, Tearfund

CHAPTER 1 — THE CALL TO JUSTICE

What's the big deal about justice?

We all have an inbuilt sense of what is fair or just. Usually it kicks in when something happens to us rather than to someone else. The other kid got the coloured crayons we wanted. Someone else got the job we should have been offered. Everyone else was going over the limit, so why did I get a ticket? But when we take our eyes off ourselves for more than a couple of minutes, we begin to see things that we don't like happening to others. Things we think are wrong, that are unjust.

I'm assuming that the reason you've picked up this book is that you have more than a passing interest in justice. Or at the very least, you are interested in why some of your Christian friends are so interested in justice. You might have used the expression 'social justice warrior' to describe someone you know. Perhaps you even worry about creeping 'political correctness' or maybe that the church is straying too far off what it should be really about, 'preaching the gospel.' Either way, I'm glad you're thinking about the issue, and picking up an introductory book like this is a good start. So take a look around you. What do you see happening at the moment? Sometimes it is a little hard to decipher what is happening in the media as there will always be a slant, and sometimes it's an ugly one. In the US you'd be forgiven for thinking that maybe there was a war on African Americans. Arguably there always has been, but recently, the Black Lives Matter movement started because of a number of high profile shooting events by police, in particular the 2012 killing of 17 year old Trayvon Martin and subsequent acquittal of the neighbourhood watch volunteer involved, George Zimmerman.[1] In Australia, the Aboriginal and Torres Strait Islander peoples lag behind non-Indigenous Australians in health, education and employment outcomes.[2]

And then there is the issue of immigration. Whether it's talk of building a wall on the US/Mexico border, describing Syrian refugees as Skittles, or banning visitors from some countries, the political rhetoric in the US has turned toxic.[3] Of course, Australia has its own strict policies, with the removal of offshore islands from our migration zone, the processing of asylum applications offshore on Manus Island and Nauru, and the refusal to settle genuine asylum seekers in Australia. As Naomi Klein noted in a 2016 visit to Australia, Donald Trump has been talking about a wall while Australia effectively has one.[4]

When it comes to economics, according to the World Bank in 2013, 767 million people lived on less than $1.90 a day. Thankfully however, this is down from 881 million in 2012 and 1.85 billion in 1990.[5] Sometimes we can make real progress on issues like poverty. And what about slavery; isn't that so 19th century? Well, the organisation Free the Slaves estimates that 21 million are enslaved worldwide, generating US$150 billion each year. About 26 per cent of all slaves are children.[6]

Hopefully you feel something when reading examples like those I've just shared. Maybe it's sorrow or a sense of lament. That would be appropriate. Maybe it's anger. Anger is such a tricky emotion. In the Sermon on the Mount, Jesus tells us that being angry with a brother or sister will be guilty before the court. He speaks of anger in the same breath as murder (Matthew 5:21-22). And yet at the same time, we see Jesus being angry at the hardness of heart of those who didn't think it right that he healed a man on the Sabbath (Mark 3:1-6). We will come back to this theme of religious dogma getting in the way of doing good shortly, but the point is that there are things which should make us angry, but without causing us to sin (Ephesians 4:26). That's the hard bit.

So the things that make us angry, the sorts of things we feel it is right to be angry about, should be things that we know are not right or just. Christians have traditionally been concerned about poverty, slavery, oppression, war, unjust treatment of the powerless and defenceless. In this book I want to add one more thing to the sorts of issues that you should think are unjust, and hopefully make you just a little bit angry about it. Climate change. And while there are many ways of framing climate change, it needs to be made very clear that unless we deal with it, all of the other issues you care about deeply will be made much, much worse.

This is not the book to convince you that climate change is real, not in the sense of sorting through the science, the reasons for accepting it, and so on. Nor is it the book to show you that you should care about climate change for its own sake, by which I mean what it is doing to the planet and the communities of plants and animals (although, see my rather brief afterword). Neither will I spend time arguing that it isn't unchristian to believe what the overwhelming majority of the climate science community are saying is happening to our home, planet Earth. I did that in my two sections of *A Climate of Hope: Church and Mission in a Warming World*, a book I wrote with my friend Claire Dawson.[7] As the name of this current book suggests, I want you to understand how climate change relates to the sorts of justice issues I listed earlier, hence a climate of justice. More than that, as the subtitle is 'loving your neighbour in a warming world', I want us to think about how we love our neighbours as ourselves in a climate that is changing, one that is making it more and more difficult to carry on with their lives as before. The focus will be on matters of justice. So before we can do that, we need to look through Scripture, albeit rather briefly, to show that justice really does matter to God.

Justice at the heart of God

There are a number of really good books on justice and the bible that you can pick up. I can't possibly hope to do justice (pun intended) to the idea of justice through the bible in one chapter. Instead, what I hope to do is simply pick out the highlights and show that justice is at the heart of both testaments, in the mind of God the Father and God the Son (and the Spirit too). Justice was for Israel and now it is for the scattered people of God throughout the world (the church).

One verse that most readers will likely be familiar with is Micah 6:8, 'He has told you, O mortal, what is good; and what does the Lord require of you but to do justice, and to love kindness, and to walk humbly with your God? (NSRV).' There are three actions that were required of Micah's readers, both the royal households and the peoples of Samaria and Jerusalem who engaged in idolatry and injustice.

The first is to do justice. Justice is not just something to talk about, or to be in love with the idea of it, as Eugene Cho often says.[8] Justice is something that is done. The word in the Hebrew translated as justice is *mishpat*. As Tim Keller discusses, *mishpat* has a range of meanings, but is often used to mean giving people their rights.[9] And by rights, I don't mean some individualistic will to power, to borrow a phrase from philosopher Friedrich Nietzsche, some libertarian ideal. Instead, rights in the bible means the opportunity to fully flourish as a human being made in the image of God (Genesis 1:26-31), to exercise dominion wisely, and to do so corporately.

Very often, these rights to flourish are applied to the most vulnerable and needy in society; widows, the fatherless, the stranger or alien, and the poor (e.g. Zechariah 7:9-11, Deuteronomy 10:17-18). It is often said that God shows preferential care for the poor, and this is not because the rich are less loveable. God so loved the world that he sent his son, not just to the poor (John 3:16). However, as Nicholas Wolterstorf notes, the poor are both more vulnerable to injustice and much more likely to suffer injustice.[10] In other words, those least likely to be able to flourish are the poor. So, *mishpat* is what we might call restorative justice; if someone is in some kind of trouble, we are called to restore them to their original state of dignity. More on this in the next chapter.

Keller also maintains that justice (*mishpat*) reflects the character of God. Justice is what God does because justice is who God is. This *mishpat* is to the oppressed, hungry, prisoners, blind, those bowed down, the just, immigrants, fatherless and widows (Psalm 146:7-9).[11] And we can see how this concern for justice continues with Jesus; doing justice is not just an Old Testament thing, it's a God thing. When Jesus read the scroll from Isaiah in the synagogue in Galilee, many of these groups were listed (Luke 4:14-21). Jesus claimed that he fulfilled this Scripture, as the one sent to preach the gospel to the poor, proclaim release to the captives, bring sight to the blind, set the oppressed free, and proclaim the Jubilee year. It is a bit hard to miss the connection; Jesus was all about kingdom justice. What is more, Jesus did these things, and could point to these things to prove to John the Baptist that he was the Messiah, Israel's long promised liberator king (Matthew 11:4-6).

What is more, even though the church now consists of people scattered throughout the world, as the people of God, we are to live justly. As God is animated by his mercy (we will get to this later) and justice, so should ours be; other focussed and giving. Jesus appears to have taught the Lord's Prayer on at least two occasions. In Matthew's version, Jesus commands to forgive our debtors (Matthew 6:12). Jesus told his followers (which includes us) to invite the poor in for dinner (Luke 14:12-13 v14). If we are peacemakers, it shows that we are those who have been blessed by God (Matthew 5:9). Paul continues this idea when he tells us to support the weak (presumably the poor) because Jesus had said it is more blessed to give than receive, an otherwise unrecorded saying. Paul himself modelled this by not taking wages for his ministry (Acts 33:35). In 2 Corinthians 8, he argues for collecting money for other churches in need based on the provision of manna in the desert wanderings of Israel. Everyone had enough to eat, no more and no less. So it should still be the case in the church. And in 1 Corinthians 6, Paul argues against lawsuits among believers, where those who are wronged and defrauded do the same thing to others. Shouldn't the church be able to sort these things out? (Note I'm not arguing here that the church shouldn't turn people over to the state in serious cases, but that that there are many things we should be able to handle internally. It's also worth being reminded that in the ancient world, as in many places today, the courts functioned best for those who could bribe the judge the most.)

At this point you might ask, isn't justice about punishment as well? Don't we talk about doing justice when someone is put in jail for his or her crimes? Don't we talk about Jesus on the cross fulfilling God's justice by receiving the punishment we deserve? Isn't part of justice punitive? And what about hell? There are some pretty big ideas here but we can't look at them all in detail. The first is to note that God does punish injustices, but steadfast or covenant love is primary (Numbers 14:18). The primary nature of love is demonstrated in the most famous verse in the whole bible; John 3:16. Salvation and not judgment is what God wants (compare verses 17-21). So while justice sometimes involves punishment, in Christ we see how restoration is the goal. Why else would he pray for those who crucified him (Luke 23:34), and command us do the same (Matthew 5:44)? Doing justice that is purely punitive is ultimately not our task, even if it is God's (Romans 9:19-20 v22).

If it is clear then that the church, like Israel, is bound to do justice within its own community, what about the outside world? Is justice only for the church itself? In the Old Testament we read that God has a concern for the injustices of the nations, and not only when they are against the people of God. Amos 1:1-2:3 forms an inward spiral of prophetic critique of the surrounding nations, before focussing in on Judah and Israel. These nations are charged for their brutality in war against each other, and they were clearly expected to remember that every human is made in God's image and therefore should be treated justly and fairly. Jesus healed a Roman Centurion's slave, who could have been Jewish, or from anywhere in the Empire (Matthew 8:5-13). Paul called the Galatians to do good to all, particularly, but not exclusively, towards those of the household of faith (Galatians 6:9-10). So justice, God's restorative *mishpat* can be extended to all who we can call neighbour, and our neighbours are all those with whom we come into contact.

Remember Micah 6:8? There are two other aspects to it to discuss briefly, before we return to the idea of doing justice. We also have to love kindness or mercy, in Hebrew *hesed*. This word is used 253 times in the Hebrew bible. In the theophany of Exodus 24, God appears before Moses and proclaims this *hesed* is fundamental to who God is. God is slow to anger and abounds in *hesed* (Numbers 14:18), *hesed* represents God's covenant faithfulness (Deuteronomy 7:9), and God's *hesed* never ceases (Lamentations 3:22). We are to love with this kind of unwavering love in doing *mishpat*. Justice is what we do, dedicated love is why we do it. You can't split justice from love, or love from justice. Justice is love made public, acted out in public. Justice without love becomes harsh and inflexible, love with justice becomes purely sentimental and indulgent.

Finally, the call to walk humbly with God reminds us that God is God, and we are not. Who deserves justice? Do the poor deserve to be poor? Very often not, but even if they did, who made you judge? Judge not, less you be judged. Be humble. As my mother often says, 'there but for the grace of God go I'. To be humble reminds us then that we often are not as loving as we should be, and can't do justice on our own without the love of God, or indeed without each other. Without God's love to guide us, our justice will always be directed to those just like us; a way too short list of those deserving of justice.

The Parable of the Good Samaritan

Luke 10:25-37 (NASB).

And a lawyer stood up and put Him to the test, saying, "Teacher, what shall I do to inherit eternal life?" And He said to him, "What is written in the Law? How does it read to you?" And he answered, "You shall love the Lord your God with all your heart, and with all your soul, and with all your strength, and with all your mind; and your neighbour as yourself." And He said to him, "You have answered correctly; do this and you will live." But wishing to justify himself, he said to Jesus, "And who is my neighbour?"

Jesus replied and said, "A man was going down from Jerusalem to Jericho, and fell among robbers, and they stripped him and beat him, and went away leaving him half dead. And by chance a priest was going down on that road, and when he saw him, he passed by on the other side. Likewise a Levite also, when he came to the place and saw him, passed by on the other side. But a Samaritan, who was on a journey, came upon him; and when he saw him, he felt compassion, and came to him and bandaged up his wounds, pouring oil and wine on them; and he put him on his own beast, and brought him to an inn and took care of him. On the next day he took out two denarii and gave them to the innkeeper and said, 'Take care of him; and whatever more you spend, when I return I will repay you.' Which of these three do you think proved to be a neighbour to the man who fell into the robbers' hands?" And he said, "The one who showed mercy toward him." Then Jesus said to him, "Go and do the same."

Being just neighbours

You may never have thought of the parable of the Good Samaritan as a parable of justice. But it is. This parable has justice written all over it. We saw earlier that justice is an overarching narrative drawn from the heart of God that unites both testaments. Doing justice sums up the law, and doing justice is love made public. The parable arose out of an argument about the law. An expert in the Mosaic Law asked Jesus about inheriting eternal life. What must he do? We tend to read about Jewish teachers of the Law as if they were Medieval Catholics trying to earn their way to heaven. In a way we should probably admire this man; at least he is trying to be part of the life of the age to come (in Greek *zôên aiônion*). Life of the age to come is a better way to read the Greek (I know, I hate people who say that sort of thing, but it justifies my study, ok?) because the phrase eternal life is often misunderstood as meaning going to heaven when you die, with a literal destruction of the physical universe. Instead, the age to come ushers in the new reign of God where, as New Testament scholar Tom Wright often likes to quote, 'the earth will be filled with the knowledge of the glory of the Lord, as the waters cover the sea' (Habakkuk 2:14). Not only does the teacher of the law get that it's about this age to come, he even nails the essence of the Law; it's about loving God with all we have and are, and loving our neighbours as ourselves. The two are linked, so full points teacher.

People worry these days about religious extremists. Prominent new atheist writer Sam Harris seems to think that religion is the ultimate justification for violence, and therefore a dangerous thing.[12] When rewards of paradise for killing the nonbeliever are on offer, religious belief is a powerful motivator for acts of violence. But Harris seems to gloss over violence done in the name of unbelief. The point isn't that religion itself is violent, but that any ideology that is not held humbly and with the needs of others in mind, i.e. a love of neighbour, will inevitably turn violent. Two points are worth making here. The first is that Harris is right when he says that religious moderates are copping out compared to extremists. It's just that he doesn't understand what a religious extremist should look like. An extremist is someone who loves, and their love of God should be absolute, all consuming. Note what the teacher of Torah says and Jesus approves of, 'You shall love the Lord your God with all your heart, and with all your soul, and with all your strength, and with all your mind (Luke 10:27)'. Love God with everything you have.

The second point to make picks up on the idea of the image of God in Genesis 1. Humans represent God to the rest of creation because we are his images. The language is cultic, i.e. the place where you would expect to find images of a deity in the Ancient Near East, and indeed in many parts of the world today, is a temple. And this is one of the reasons that Old Testament scholar John Walton believes that the creation should be viewed as a temple.[13] This act of sanctifying or making holy all of creation as a divine temple removes the barrier between secular and sacred spaces, or secular and sacred vocations, an idea we will examine more soon. So, if we are to love God, shouldn't we also love humans who are made in his image? The teacher of Torah quickly adds to his summary of the need to love God with 'and your neighbour as yourself.' One follows directly from the other. Such an idea is reflected in the prohibition of murder in Genesis 9, based on humans being made in God's image (Genesis 1). Yet behind this command to refrain from murder is the deeper command to love. Do the just thing (don't murder) because it is the loving thing to do. Love God, and because you love God, love your neighbour.

Of course, the idea of neighbour can be used rather restrictively. There is an old saying that 'charity begins at home,' usually said by those for whom it ends there as well. Yet as we shall see, the parable points to the fact that our neighbour is the one whom we encounter going about our daily lives. So you might think I've just contradicted myself. How do we encounter people? I'll say more about this later, but I'd like to include a quote from an address I gave at the climate change rally in Melbourne in 2013, organised by the campaigning organisation GetUp!

> In a world where I wear clothes made in Bangladesh, watch American movies on a Korean TV, and when I drive my Japanese car I add gases that warm the whole planet, **everyone** is my neighbour. In the parable of the Good Samaritan, Jesus told a story about a man attacked by robbers, to teach us that we are to love our neighbours when they are in need.

Yes I realise it is kind of pretentious to quote myself (pretentious? Moi?), but I think the point I was making is a valid one, that we live in both an interconnected global economy and an interconnected planet.

We share the same economy and the same ecological system – and funnily enough both words derive from the Greek word *oikos*, meaning household. You can't have an economy without ecology, and we share both with seven or so billion other people. Everyone is my neighbour, and so while I may have special responsibility to love those nearest to me, there is no avoiding my need of those to whom I am not near, thanks to my purchases or lifestyle. More of that in the last chapter.

For some Christians, it might be ok to understand that everyone is my neighbour, but isn't my highest and most important calling to love my neighbour by sharing the gospel with them? Shouldn't I be letting people know that because God so loved the world, that Jesus died for people's sins (John 3:16)? Isn't social justice a distraction from the main game of the church? Think about that famous passage, Matthew 28:18-20, the Great Commission. As a Christian I believe we need to take the Great Commission seriously, to take mission more seriously. Church is often structured, as missiologists Michael Frost and Alan Hirsch note in their book *The Shaping of Things to Come*, around the people already there and not the people we are trying to reach. [14] But there are a few important things to note about the Great Commission.

The first is the idea of all authority being given to Jesus, in heaven and on *earth* (Matthew 28:18). This is the fulfilment of the Lord's Prayer; the kingdom has come in Jesus and through him and the church, God's will is done on *earth* as it is in heaven. This all-encompassing authority means that Jesus is not just about the church and its four walls, not just about 'spiritual' things, but has authority over all things. The fact that the gospel is about the kingdom of God should tell us something about what the gospel content will look like and the results of proclaiming the gospel. Jesus has come, as Tom Wright often says, to put the world to rights. Things are out of shape, be they individual human hearts, political systems, financial systems, multinational companies, courts, and our relationship with the non-human creation. All this needs putting right. Israel was God's servant, and as such was to be a light to the nations (Isaiah 49:6). Jesus as that servant shone light into the darkness (John 1:5). The vocation of the church then is to be light to the darkness, proclaiming the Good News. That means walking in dark places, getting our hands dirty.

Some Christians might argue that it is enough to preach repentance and everything else will sort itself out. But while corrupt structures remain untouched, old injustices remain. What is more, we tend to draw false distinctions between public and private sin. So we might condemn gluttony (although when did you last hear a sermon against it?) but do we protest about the fact that so much food is wasted globally each year while people go hungry? As individuals we believe we should turn the other cheek, but what about unjust wars or illegal assassinations by drone? If greed is bad, why do we sit and let large companies pay no tax, underpay workers and overpay CEOs?

Another thing to note about the Great Commission is that Jesus asked his disciples to make disciples. Conversion is not enough, discipleship is a lifelong process of observing in life all that Jesus commanded them. The failure to do this is what Dallas Willard has called 'The Great Omission.'[15] When we read the Sermon on the Mount, we need to understand that the virtues present are not an optional extra, much less a way of ensuring we 'stay on the bus' and make it to heaven when we die. Instead, the Sermon on the Mount is a manifesto of kingdom values, what the kingdom come on earth should look like. Even just restricting ourselves to the Beatitudes we can see the theme of justice running through them. Those who hunger for righteousness will be satisfied. Of course, some Christians read righteousness as personal attributes of holiness. While it is true that we need to be morally upright, the concept of righteousness is broader than this, and is captured by one Greek word *dikaiosune* (pronounced dik-ah-yos-oo'-nay). This word can also be translated as justice.[16] The idea of peacemaking only makes sense in a social context where conflict has arisen, spanning our personal relations all the way up to global conflicts. Likewise, while it is true that people are persecuted for religious belief, is it because they exhibit sound personal qualities, those of religious righteousness, or because they stand up for justice? Hopefully the point is clear; personal righteousness and public justice are on the same continuum and are part of our discipleship.

So in turning to the Great Commission, we come to realise that justice is part and parcel of our disciple making. Again, if we lack love, we only focus on people's sins and not their physical needs. James had powerful words to say against this. This is dead faith! (James 2:14-17) So if we preach a gospel where we separate forgiveness from restoration and wholeness, we preach a dead gospel. The Hebrew word that captures this idea of wholeness is *shalom*. Shalom is usually translated in English as peace, but it isn't merely the absence of conflict. As Tim Keller points out, shalom represents complete reconciliation and full flourishing.[17] In the Hebrew Bible (the Christian Old Testament), this shalom was freedom from war with neighbours, long life, a land flowing with milk and honey, and the blessing of many children. In the New Testament, shalom is I think what Jesus is getting at in John 10:10, about having life to the full. While we can fall into so-called prosperity gospel thinking, equating fullness of life solely with the abundance of possessions and wealth, we can go too far the other way of falling for an austere gospel that lacks vitality and joy.

So does the parable of the Good Samaritan have anything to offer us on the idea of separating forgiveness from true shalom? I believe it does; a rather uncomfortable point. We are so used to reading the various religious figures of the New Testament in a negative light, and fail to identify with them. Sometimes it is more a case, I think, of profoundly misguided individuals trying to do the right thing, and we must identify with that aspect in ourselves.

Recall the fate of the nameless man in the parable of the Good Samaritan. He was stripped, beaten and left for dead. So why did the priest and the Levite, coming from some holy duty in Jerusalem, ignore his plight? Well firstly, as one stripped, we don't know if it was naked or not, the man was shamefully exposed. Remember in Genesis 2-3, in the garden the man and woman initially knew no shame, but later became aware that they were naked and felt ashamed. We have fewer scruples about nudity these days, but we still understand shame more than we think. Personal hygiene is still the norm in polite society. When did you last approach a homeless person and found it had been a while since they last bathed? Did you find this an issue? Likewise, some people are ashamed of being in need and having to ask for help, and we can share that awkwardness. America has that can do attitude, which can be a real positive. However, the flip side of this, as the philosopher Alain de Botton uncovers in his book and accompanying TV series *Status Anxiety,* is that a can do culture of success can also lead us to shame and blame those who aren't as successful as us.[18] The idea that the poor deserve it affects our thinking, especially when applied to ethnic minorities or a nation's First People.

The second reason for inaction on the part of the Levite and priest is that the man was beaten half to death. Did he simply look dead? Well the Law had a good out for that, a corpse made you unclean (Numbers 19:11-13, Leviticus 22:4). We know that ritual cleanliness had become an obsession in the first century. Archaeological digs in Jerusalem have uncovered rich priestly houses with multiple baths for ritual bathing. This is what the Law prescribed. In one sense, the priest and Levite were doing the right thing. Yet we also know in a far more important way, they were missing the point of the Law. A focus on being completely right before the Law in its ritual requirements led to missing out on what was more important. To be sure, there were ways of being made clean again, it's not like it would be permanent! No, what was lacking in both of these characters was compassion, the compassion that the Samaritan felt (Luke 10:33). This same word is used to describe what Jesus felt when he saw the crowds following him, distressed like sheep without a shepherd (Matthew 9:36).

People have a tendency not to stop and help others when they are busy, as a university study showed.[19] Our lives have become very busy, and we come up with many excuses not to stop and help. The worst sort are religious excuses: those who think they should busy themselves only with Evangelism, viewed in a very narrow way, those who worry about becoming contaminated by 'liberal doctrine' or some such. I don't mean to sound harsh, and it is true that people have different gifts and callings. Not everyone is called to be a professional in the area of justice advocacy, foreign aid, and so on. And yet we are all called to compassion, with hands, hearts and wallets. There is no good theological argument not to find ways of doing acts of justice.

Working for justice with neighbours

In the last section, we looked at the idea of loving your neighbour as justice, looking at the parable of the Good Samaritan. We finished with the idea that we shouldn't be afraid of being 'contaminated.' To be sure, good doctrine is important, but not at the expense of compassion. The two should fit together. And the more comfortable we are with our beliefs, the more we should be willing to work with others of different beliefs, not less.

One of the things that the parable points out to us is that Jesus expects our love of neighbour to cross boundaries. People blithely use the label Good Samaritan without realising the profound divide between Jew and Samaritan. The Samaritans were regarded as pariahs by the Jews, like illegitimate half-siblings. After the ten northern tribes were carried away into captivity by the Assyrians in about 720 BC, peoples from other parts of the empire were settled there (2 Kings 17:24). These people kept their own religious beliefs as well as worshipping the God of Israel. The Samaritans had their own temple on Mount Gerizim, and only accepted the first five books of the Hebrew bible as sacred. Jews had no dealings with Samaritans (John 4:9). In holding up a Samaritan as an example of neighbour love to a Jewish religious leader, Jesus was being very provocative. More than that, he was calling us to break down all barriers in the pursuit of loving our neighbour.

This of course means that we do justice to anyone and everyone, and as I pointed out earlier, we live in a global village where everyone is our neighbour in one way or another. But what about crossing boundaries to work with others? You might argue that it is one thing to work or volunteer for a Christian aid and advocacy agency like Micah or TEAR, but not for a secular one. And didn't Paul tell us not to be unequally yoked or bound (2 Corinthians 6:14)? Theologian Ernest Best in his commentary on 2 Corinthians points out that the pressing issue for the Greek believers in Corinth, who were converts from Greco-Roman religion, was that they might fall again under the influence of idols.[20] Many of the idols of today that we face are not of stone and wood, and there is a danger of distraction for us from the centrality of the gospel. But, Best warns, we run the risk of Pharisaism if we obsess over being separate from the world to the exclusion of working in the world. Tom Wright thinks the most obvious subject of 2 Corinthians 6:14 is marriage; this in itself is a theological hand grenade and thankfully need not occupy us here.[21] The point is, one can be in the world, working with the world for justice based on shared ideas, yet not be of the world, having our own central convictions shaped and moulded by the gospel.

It is also worth noting that people of all beliefs have an understanding of what is just and unjust. We might not agree on every detail, and certainly not on the basis of such ideas. Best points out that Christian values had, and perhaps still in some cases have, an influence on western thinking. Likewise, Paul can say on one hand that no one is righteous (Romans 3:10) and yet that people show that the Law is written on their consciences (Romans 2:14-15). I go over this even though to some of us it should be obvious, so that when we come to a document like the Sustainable Development Goals (SDGs), we should see them for what they are, admirable goals that reflect biblical ideas of justice. Some Christians want to hold the UN at arm's length, with some even applying fanciful thinking about 'world government' and the mark of the beast to the UN, based on a literalistic reading of the book of Revelation. I believe such thinking is misguided on many levels, and there's not much space to unpack this here, other than to say that good governance is a gift from God, and that global governance, and not global government, is what many UN bodies are about. Christians can work with others to try to achieve the aims of the SDGs, not because we believe we will establish a utopia, heaven on earth as it were. We believe that heaven has established a beachhead on earth, and those of us in Christ, who Paul refers to as those having the first fruits of the Spirit (Romans 8:23), are it!

The list of SDGs includes traditional Christian interests such as ending poverty and hunger, providing education, clean water and sanitation, good health, gender equality, and economic equality.[22] To back this up, it also calls for good infrastructure, without which none of this is achievable. The goals also acknowledge the role of partnerships, and so there's plenty of room for Christians to become involved. Several goals also relate to the environment, including action on climate change.

The main argument of this book is that if we don't deal with climate change, all of our other justice concerns will be affected.

The rest of this book will look at a small selection of justice issues, and their relationship to climate change. It's a selective list but is illustrative of the general idea. In chapter 2, we look at the idea of aid and justice. What good do our dollars do when we give to development projects overseas? What impacts does reduction in aid have? What about the need to fund climate change adaption projects? In chapter 3, we will look at the issue of modern slavery, and how climate change is helping drive it in countries like India. Chapter 4 will examine the issue of refugees and asylum seekers, and how climate change is already causing people to be displaced, let alone how sea level rise will affect migration in future. Chapter 5 will look at the gap between Aboriginal and Torres Strait Islander peoples and non-indigenous Australians, and how climate change will likely widen this gap. In the last chapter, we will return to the parable of the Good Samaritan and dig into its backstory. This will help us understand how dealing with the symptoms of climate change is important, and that dealing with the issue itself and our own place in it, is unavoidable. There's also a brief afterword, where I seek to stretch your thinking just that little bit further.

Endnotes

1 *Black Lives Matter*, accessed 4 February, 2017, http://blacklivesmatter.com/about/.

2 Australian Government, Department of the Prime Minister and Cabinet, *Closing the Gap*, accessed 4 February, 2017, http://closingthegap.dpmc.gov.au/. See also chapter 5.

3 Christine Hauser, "Donald Trump Jr. compares Syrian refugees to Skittles that 'would kill you'," *The New York Times,* September 20, 2016, accessed December 21, 2016, http://www.nytimes.com/2016/09/21/us/politics/donald-trump-jr-faces-backlash-after-comparing-syrian-refugees-to-skittles-that-can-kill.html.

4 Michael Slezak, "Q&A: Naomi Klein criticizes Institute for Public Affairs over climate interventions," *The Guardian*, 8 November, 2016, accessed 4 February 2017, https://www.theguardian.com/australia-news/2016/nov/08/qa-naomi-klein-criticises-australias-climate-and-asylum-policies.

5 World Bank, "Poverty Overview, updated 2 October, 2016, accessed 4 February, 2017, http://www.worldbank.org/en/topic/poverty/overview.

6 Free the Slaves, "Slavery is Everywhere," accessed 4 February, 2017, http://www.freetheslaves.net/about-slavery/slavery-today/.

7 Claire Dawson and Mick Pope, *A Climate of Hope: Church and Mission in a Warming*

World (Melbourne: UNOH Publishing, 2014).

8 Eugene Cho, *Overrated: Are We More in Love with the Idea of Changing the World Than Actually Changing the World?* (Colorado Springs, CO: David C. Cook, 2014).

9 Timothy Keller, *Generous Justice: How God's Grace Makes Us Just* (New York: Dutton, 2010), 3.

10 Cited in Keller, *Generous Justice*, 7.

11 Keller, *Generous Justice*, 5.

12 Sam Harris, *The End of Faith: Religion, Terror, and the Future of Reason* (New York: W. H. Norton, 2005).

13 John Walton, *The Lost World of Genesis One: Ancient Cosmology and the Origin Debate* (Nottingham: IVP Academic, 2009).

14 Michael Frost and Alan Hirsch, *The Shaping of Things to Come: Innovation and Mission for the 21st Century Church* (Peabody, MA: Hendrickson Publishing, 2003).

15 Dallas Willard, *The Great Omission: Reclaiming Jesus' Essential Teachings on Discipleship* (San Francisco: Harper One, 2014).

16 Frederick William Danker, *A Greek-English Lexicon of the New Testament and Other Early Christian Literature* (Chicago: The University of Chicago Press, 2000), 247.

17 Tim Keller, *Generous Justice*, 174.

18 Alain de Botton, *Status Anxiety* (London: Penguin Books, 2004).

19 Darley, J. M., and Batson, C.D., ""From Jerusalem to Jericho": A study of Situational and Dispositional Variables in Helping Behavior," *Journal of Personality and Social Psychology*, 27 (1973): 100-108.

20 Ernest Best, *Second Corinthians: Interpretation, A Bible Commentary for Teaching and Preaching* (Louisville, Kentucky: Westminster John Knox Press, 2012), 65-68.

21 Tom Wright, *Paul for Everyone: Second Corinthians* (London: SPCK, 2003), 74.

22 United Nations, "Department of Economic and Social Affairs, Sustainable Development Knowledge Platform," accessed 4 February, 2017, https://sustainabledevelopment.un.org/sdgs.

Chapter 2 — Money makes the world go around

Money, money, money

How many songs you can name that talk about money? Liza Minelli sang that 'money makes the world go around.' In 1976, the Swedish supergroup ABBA sang about life in a rich man's world, and how easy is must be. Yes, I'm showing my age. More sinisterly, in 1987 the British pop band Hollywood reminded us that riches come at a cost. The song 'What's the colour of money?' tells us that money dulls our senses and denies our principles. Its colour is not green but red. Notorious B.I.G commented that the 'more money we come across the more problems we see.' Now of course Paul was very careful to tell us that it is love of money, not money itself that is the root of all evil (1 Timothy 6:10), so we mustn't be over negative about what is a useful tool. Indeed, the right use of money is the whole point of this chapter. Once we've examined the positive role that thoughtful aid can play, and why it is important for foreign aid to increase, I will stress how even more important aid is in a warming world.

Aid works

Consider for a moment the small island nation of East Timor, or Timor-Leste. Timor-Leste is a former Portuguese colony, which briefly gained independence in 1975. A revolution in Portugal led to all of its former colonies being granted independence. In December of 1975, Indonesia invaded East Timor with minimal comment from Australia. There were concerns over the left leaning nature of the political party Fretilin, who were thought to be Communist.[1] It also appears the case that a pragmatic approach to obtaining access to Timorese oil and gas played a role, as Australian ambassador to Indonesia Richard Woolcott stated at the time; 'The present gap in the agreed seabed border … could be much more readily negotiated with Indonesia … than with Portugal or an independent Portuguese Timor. I know I am recommending a pragmatic rather than a principled stand but that is what the national interest and foreign policy is all about.'[2]

In 1999, after over 20 years of occupation, the Timorese were given a free vote on independence from Indonesia, with over 78% responding in the positive. The actions of pro-integration groups that followed, was, in the words of the Senate Foreign Affairs report, a 'campaign of violence, killings, massive looting and destruction of property and infrastructure, forced transportation of large numbers of people to West Timor and the flight of most of the rest of the population from their homes, left the East Timor economy in ruin.'[3]

The Senate Foreign Affairs report also noted that Timor-Leste had been at the bottom of every indicator of poverty while part of Indonesia, including infant nutrition.[4] Sustainable Development Goals (SDGs) two and three refer to eliminating hunger and promoting good health. Malnutrition is still a problem in Timor-Leste, but gains are being made. Take for example the story of Jovandro, who lives with his mother Adriana de Andrade in the village of Lontale. When he was one, Jovandro was malnourished, underweight and often sick. He was raised on a diet of rice porridge. By the time he was five, Jovandro was healthy and active, and his younger sibling was enjoying a healthier infancy than he had. The difference? Oxfam Australia educated his mother on a better diet that avoids malnutrition, one where eggs and vegetables were included in his rice meals.[5] This simple program of education is a wonderful example of how aid can be supplied in a practical manner. More than that, education is life-changing and allows people to flourish under their own efforts, maintaining their dignity.

Aid achieves positive outcomes. According to Micah Australia, Australian aid in 2015 vaccinated 2.3 million children (SDG 3), gave 2.9 million people access to clean water (SDG 6), built 9,000 classrooms (SDG 4), funded skilled birth attendants for 1 million births (SDG 2), provide support and services to 66,000 women who survived violence (SDG 5), supported more than 400,000 farmers with better technology (SDG 3, 11), and gave life-saving support to Syrian refugees, whole communities recovering from Typhoon Haiyan in the Philippines, and the Nepal earthquake.[6] Aid can help eliminate diseases like small pox, saving 200 million lives. Insecticide treated mosquito nets help reduce the incidence of malaria and associated deaths.[7]

Tightening other people's belts

All of these are amazing achievements. All of them helping communities get back on their feet, or providing essential health services to help people survive and flourish, to learn and to feed themselves. All of them are enabling. This is what aid can do. Sadly, when governments look to tighten their belts, it is usually those who are least able to afford it, both domestically and overseas, who end up paying the price. Robin Davies of the Development Policy Centre and the Australian National University comments that Australia has now moved into a class of its own when it comes to foreign aid cuts.[8] The United Nations set a target for OECD countries to give at least 0.7% of their gross national income as foreign aid by 2015, as part of the Millennium project.[9] Six countries: Denmark, Luxembourg, the Netherlands, Norway, Sweden and the UK have met their goals. In 2015, 22 of the 28 OECD donor countries had increased their spending. Australia meanwhile has continued to cut its giving. In 2015 it was just above the median value for OECD countries. Spending has fallen from 0.36% in 2012 to 0.23% in 2016. Meanwhile, the US is at less than 0.2%, admittedly given its much larger budget, the US gives way more in absolute terms. The Australian public gives about one quarter of what the Australian government does, with agencies in 2014-15 receiving donations from 1.64 million individuals.[10]

While US foreign aid is large, it is a small percentage of its total budget. Obama's proposed 2017 budget allocated $50.1 billion out of a total budget of $4.15 trillion. Of that aid budget, $8.1 billion is military aid that usually includes spending the money on American manufactured arms (except in the case of Israel).[11] Economic aid and development money is shared around many poorer African nations, but America's largest giving is to Afghanistan, whose economy has been ravaged by war. Now that we are in the age of 'America first' under President Trump, what will become of American foreign aid? Trump has variously said 'It is necessary that we invest in our infrastructure, stop sending foreign aid to countries that hate us and use that money to rebuild our tunnels, roads, bridges and schools,' and 'at what point do you say, hey, we have to take care of ourselves.' He has, however, promised to take the lead on fighting AIDS. There is an interesting mismatch between public perception and reality, with many believing that spending on development and public health it is over 20%![12] This is a shared theme with Australia. A 2016 poll found that for a sample size of about 1500 Australians, the average perception was that Australian foreign aid giving was about 13% of the budget. The same group of people recommended that about 10% would be a fair amount.[13]

So why is the Australian government reducing foreign aid, when there has been past bipartisan support for reaching the 0.7% target? A report by the Lowry Institute for International Policy discusses the decline in aid.[14] Four years of cuts now sees the aid budget 30% under what it was under the Labor government in 2012/13, including a 20% slashing in 2015. The argument made by government was the need for austerity to deal with a budget deficit, but as the report points out, government expenditure increased by 9.3% while aid was cut by 30%. Rather telling is the statement made in 2014 by the treasurer at the time, Joe Hockey, that 'Defence and national security commitments totalling $1.3 billion are more than offset by savings in our foreign aid Budget of $3.7 billion. Where we have made savings we have worked hard to ensure that there will be no negative impact on the Australian economy.'[15] It seems that the government sees beefing up national security as important enough to cut aid and development needs for our neighbours. This is somewhat ironic, because moving money from foreign aid into arms in order to improve national security ignores the fact that foreign aid can deliver political stability to a region.[16] It also seems curious that the tax base from which aid and other programs are funded doesn't include the scrapped mining tax, price on carbon, or tax avoidance by the so-called 1%.[17]

Spending like good neighbours

As we turn to the parable of the Good Samaritan (Luke 10:30-37), we need to consider the value of money very carefully. Money is given a prominent role in this parable, but it is often too easy to overlook it. In thinking about what the parable says about money, we need to look at how it is described, which is quite explicit, but then also think carefully about what it is for, which might not be quite as obvious. Firstly, we might ask what our hypothetical Samaritan would have been doing on the road to Jerusalem. Was he on business? What business could a man, that every Jew he passed would have despised, possibly have? But unlike the others, he felt compassion and stopped what he was doing (verse 33). They say time is money, and we are pretty keen to spend it on ourselves. We busy ourselves so much with our various activities, often doing overtime with work or that extra shift or job, just to stay ahead. Yet whatever economic activity the Samaritan was engaged in, he stopped for this Jew, his supposed enemy. I wonder sometimes if you feel as I do, and justify to yourself not stopping to give a few coins to someone living on the street because you are in a hurry to get to work?

While we place an emphasis on money itself, we also need to think about our possessions and their use. It is easy enough to give away clothes that are old and worn, maybe less so for things that might still be new, but we no longer need. The Samaritan takes time to bandage up the man's wounds (verse 34). Now unless he had a St John's ambulance first aid kit, I'm not sure where the bandages came from. Perhaps from his own clothes? I doubt there was much of the victim's clothes from which to make bandages. Regardless, the Samaritan (I wish he had a name; I'm tempted to call him Sam), provided out of his own material. He also used oil and wine on the wounds. Today we know that wine, especially red wine, has antiseptic properties. The Roman physicians Celsus in the second century BC and Galen in the second century AD both wrote about its use for this purpose.[18] Celsus describes how, after the bleeding has been suppressed, if the patient cannot bear the strength of vinegar, wine should be applied to the wound.[19] Now I'm not suggesting the next time little Johnny skins his knee, you whip out the chardonnay or pinot noir. The point is this; justice costs in time and resources.

There is also effort in doing good. The Samaritan took his own beast, gave up his own ride, to carry the man to an inn. We are to imagine that this was necessary. The man had been left for dead, and was probably not in a fit state to give his consent to be treated, let alone walk to an inn. If you have done first aid training, you might be familiar with the acronym DRS ABCD. The D stands for danger. We will come back to this more in the last chapter, but the obvious question to ask was, were there more bandits about? Is it safe to offer help? The R stands for response. I'm guessing in this case there was none; the man was incapacitated, possibly barely conscious. We might live in an age where people sue you left, right and centre, and offering help can be risky. The Samaritan just jumped right in. And given that there was no ambulance to send for help to (the S in the acronym), the Samaritan took the man to an inn himself, to care for him (verse 34).

So through this process, the Samaritan has spent time and resources. But given that he put himself and the man up in the inn, there was some initial expense as well. Money changed hands. Maybe the Samaritan would have stopped at the inn anyway; maybe he would have pushed on back to Samaria for a possibly friendlier welcome. In the telling of this parable, Jesus leaves us with so many unanswered questions, and we risk pushing details too far. But there's a real first century world of conflict behind the text, and the questions are worth asking. We then see another financial transaction take place. The Samaritan hands over two denarii, two silver Roman coins which were two days' wages for a labourer. This was not the kind of small change you might pop into a donation tin. There is a financial transaction and a financial risk. Will these coins be spent on the needs of the man left in the innkeeper's care? And will the appropriate extra expenses be charged when the Samaritan returns? Will the innkeeper skim off the top? Whatever the case, the Samaritan offers to repay whatever the innkeeper spends on the man (verses 35).

So what have we learned so far about doing justice? It often takes money. It can take a lot of money and it needs to be provided in a sustainable fashion. What should be obvious, but needs to be stated as we come to think about aid and investment is that aid dollars need to be spent where they are needed, rather than where donors want it spent. This involves a process of consultation. Think about Jesus' interaction with Bartimaeus in Mark 10. Jesus asks him 'What do you want me to do for you?' (v51, NASB). The patient in the parable needs medical attention, food and shelter. This is what the Samaritan provided him with. This links to a second idea. We know nothing about the victim, other than he was in need. The man would have had a job of some sort. Maybe he was an artisan. Maybe he had his own land to provide for his family. The point is that we, like him, all have lives that we live. Being beset by robbers means that this man was being kept from carrying out his normal state of affairs, from spending time with the people he liked. He had a life to go back to. Like any hospital patient, he would be waiting for the time when he could go home, not spending the rest of his days at the inn being cared for. This might seem like an obvious point to make, but it allows us to take one step further when we think about the goals of aid.

Aid is not about the giver, but the receiver. Besides, the Samaritan man had his own life to go on with and was no doubt keen to get back to whatever he was doing before he came across the wounded man. However, as we have seen, he made sufficient provision for the wounded man with the promise of more money if it was needed. He didn't stick around for a selfie, or a quick Facebook post about his short-term mission trip to Israel. It wasn't about him. It was about the Jewish man and his recovery to normal life. Aid shouldn't be designed to set up dependency between receiver and donor, but instead should allow people to flourish with dignity and independence. Disaster relief is an act of *mishpat* because its intention is to return people to where they were before. Think, for example, of the humanitarian aid given to Sri Lanka after the Boxing Day Tsunami of 2001. Disaster relief represents less than 15% of total overseas aid given in 2015 by OECD countries.[20]

However, most aid is given to help poorer countries develop and raise the quality of people's lives. The Sustainable Development Goals highlight a number of areas where aid should be targeted, including poverty, hunger, clean water and sanitation. This is also *mishpat* in the sense that aid tries to level the playing field, giving people opportunities they would not otherwise have. We might consider why that might be, but for now, given that we believe that all humans were created in the image of God, it makes sense that gross inequality is not something to be tolerated because it represents the injustice of not sharing the resources of the earth, or worse. Furthermore, given that the inequality of global markets is the legacy (at least in part) of colonialism, we should have extra motivation to get people to a place where they have the opportunity to flourish.

This is probably the time to address a question that I see raised often in discussions about foreign aid, even among Christians. Surely we should look to our own first. Why spend money on foreign aid when so many young people and families in Australia are homeless? Why help farmers overseas when our own farmers are struggling, with high rates of suicide? There seems to be a never-ending need domestically, so why would we invest resources elsewhere? The first response would be, why is giving aid a zero sum game? Particularly for Christians, why are love and justice things that can somehow be exhausted? This not to ignore the fact that money is finite, but simply poses the question why it is we should wait until every last one of our problems are solved before we look overseas. The second answer to such a question would be from the parable itself. We are reminded that our love of God is demonstrated in our love of neighbour; one flows out of the other. You might say that we see Jesus in the stranger in need, which is pretty much the point of Matthew 25 and the parable of the sheep and the goats. To be a Christian is to be generous, not miserly. To be a Christian is to be called to love those from very different walks of life, even those who we might deem enemies. So what good argument is there to stop our personal overseas giving, or demanding that our tax dollars be used for the benefit of the global poor? Thirdly, and related to the second point, might we ask about how much money is available to spend, and how the decisions on spending the money are made. Given that government spending on aid comes from taxes, how are those taxes collected, and from whom? If money is an issue in rich countries like Australia, the UK or USA, something must be wrong! We'll return to this point later.

Spending wisely in a warming world

Developing a sustainable economy includes guaranteeing food security. Sustainable Development Goal 2 is to eliminate hunger. Feeding a growing global population is a challenge. There are an ever-increasing number of mouths globally, and rising affluence is usually associated with larger meat consumption. All of this means more land and/or more intensive forms of farming. There is only so much land available to convert to farmland, and this happens at the expense of land, which is important for a number of other issues, including conservation of biodiversity, water purification, and natural resources. In many parts of the world, these resources include timber, bush food, and natural medicines. On top of all of this, climate change is already having an impact on staple crops like wheat and maize. The Synthesis Report of the Fifth Assessment Report of the Intergovernmental Panel on Climate Change (IPCC) observed that 'many studies covering a wide range of regions and crops shows that negative impacts of climate change on crop yields have been more common than positive impacts (high confidence).'[21] The future scenarios of carbon dioxide emissions that the IPCC uses to model future climates are known as Representative Concentration Pathways or RCPs. Given current trends in carbon dioxide emissions, we are currently on track for the highest emission scenario (RCP 8.5). Under this scenario, there are potentially large impacts on global crop yields by the 2080s, including up to 45% of global average yield losses for maize compared to the 1980s, up to 52% reduction for spring wheat, and up to 25% for soybean.[22]

Coming back to Australian aid then, it turns out that the environment doesn't feature very highly in the figures, at about 1% of spending. Of OECD countries in 2015, spending on environmental sustainability amounted to about 5% of aid. Issues like environmental sustainability are referred to as cross cutting measures, spanning a number of different areas. As a result, they are not captured perfectly in OECD reporting. A recent Oxfam report documents how little actually reaches the ground for climate adaptation. In 2013, only 25% of the $52.2 billion OECD said was mobilised toward climate grants, a mere $13 billion. Of that figure, only $1.5 billion was dedicated to climate change adaptation.[23]

Aid needs to be driven by local context and not by specific issues, but as climate change continues to impact all of the issues to which aid is normally addressed, it will have to become more prominent in aid spending budgets. And as Ben Clark of TEAR told me, there are no easy answers as to how a small-scale project can really respond given the limited data scope and timeframe of most projects. Sustained spending at multiple scales, in a coordinated fashion, would make most sense.

Herein lies the importance of the Green Climate Fund, managed under the United Nations Framework Convention on Climate Change.

The stated aims of this fund are to 'make a significant and ambitious contribution towards the global efforts to combat climate change.'[24] This effort consists of low carbon emission projects, aimed at mitigating the impacts of climate change, and programs aimed at developing resilience, i.e. adaptation. The target countries are the least developed countries, Small Island Developing States (SIDS) and African States. However, the Oxfam report mentioned earlier recommends that the Green Climate Fund needs to focus on programmatic approaches 'needed to scale up adaptation actions that support the most vulnerable women and men at the local level', rather than on a project by project basis.[25]

Mitigation projects are aimed at reducing carbon emissions via changes in land use and protection of forests, transport infrastructure, energy generation and access, buildings, city design, and industries. Issues like transport and city design are important given the global trend to urbanisation, which is happening most rapidly in the developing world. For example, in Africa it is expected that the percentage of people living in urban areas will increase from about 40% in 2014 to nearly 60% in 2050.[26] Adaptation focuses on increasing the resilience of health, food and water security, livelihoods of communities and people, ecosystems and ecosystem services, and infrastructure and the built environment.[27] Adaptation spending to date has mostly focussed on water management, whereas mitigation has focussed mostly on renewable energy.[28]

Renewable energy is of particular interest in the developing world, quite apart from climate mitigation efforts. In 2010, over 1 billion people worldwide were without electricity. This number includes nearly 90% of people in Sub-Saharan Africa and South Asia, those mostly living in rural areas.[29] About 300 million of the people without access to electricity live in rural India. With India the third largest emitter of greenhouse gases, connecting these people to renewable sources of energy is a matter of justice for them and future generations.[30]

Spending on climate mitigation and adaptation is particularly important for Sub-Saharan Africa and SIDS. Climate change is projected to cost SIDS 1% of gross domestic product (GDP), which is five times higher than the global average. Africa is expected to bear the brunt of adaptation costs, nearly 50% of health, water supply, and agriculture and forestry costs, while representing only one seventh of the world's population.[31] This is hardly a just arrangement!

Given the high costs involved in climate change adaptation and mitigation for poorer countries, it is important to have targeted aid, although it is likely that these areas will overlap with aid funded by other means. Thankfully, the Australian Federal Government has shown its support for the Green Development Fund. In late 2014, it announced a $200 million commitment to the Fund. This commitment represented a change of mind for the then Prime Minister Tony Abbott. Mr Abbott described the amount as 'modest, prudent and proportionate.' However, the Climate Institute believes it falls short of what we should be giving, and Oxfam says it is just the beginning.[32] In 2017, Australia leads the Green Development Fund.[33] By way of contrast, the situation in the US is more uncertain. Under President Obama, the US donated $1 billion dollars to the Fund, half of which was signed off by Obama just three days before he left office.[34] President Trump has made various pronouncements about climate change, none convincingly affirming of its existence. Support of the Fund needs to be bipartisan, continual and large. The costs to developing nations in the future without adaptation and mitigation spending now will be enormous, making the SDGs discussed in chapter one much more difficult to achieve.

Campaigning for justice on Aid
Giving like good neighbours

Hopefully by now you can see the value of spending like a good neighbour, and can see that maybe we are not. There are ways in which you can get behind this by giving to organisations that invest well in the lives of others. What follows can't possibly hope to be comprehensive, but reflects some of the things I've been involved with, or at least have a passing interest in.

The TEAR Australia Really Useful Gift catalogue is a practical way to challenge the materialist thinking that surrounds Christmas, raise awareness of development needs in other countries, and actually supports people with things that they need. You select a card featuring a photo and name of the gift you have purchased, plus space inside for you to write a personal message. On the back of the card is a short description of TEAR's work, a description of the item you've purchased as it appears online and a caption for the photo. Every gift you buy from TEAR's Useful Gifts represents a contribution to a long-term development project, helping people gain the skills and resources they need to address local problems and come up with sustainable solutions.

Imagine buying a goat or a toilet for your favourite in-law! Well, in reality, your purchase of a specific gift is representative of the type of community development work done by TEAR projects. For example, the purchase of a toilet helps to support the work of TEAR's Water and Sanitation projects. These projects may well install toilets, but they also provide training and education in hygiene, safe water practices, and maintenance of equipment, such as wells and water systems. Likewise, a goat contributes to Livelihoods and Food Security programs, where communities are provided the skills and tools to transform their lives through better agriculture techniques, training and resources. Some projects will provide goats, and other animals, but they are part of a wider picture of community development.

For more information see https://www.usefulgifts.org/.

Direct giving is also an option. You can donate to an aid organisation and let them decide how to spend it. Remember that aid should always be directed by need. Even for the Really Useful Gift catalogue, if one item is oversubscribed, your purchase money can be redirected to similar areas. For UK readers, the TEARFund website has a really helpful pie chart to show how funds are allocated. For more information see http://www.tearfund.org/en/give/.

Child sponsorship is another way of giving. My wife and I have sponsored children via Child Fund since we were first married, seeing young Wilson through school and into a trade apprenticeship. We now have two others from Ecuador and Sierra Leone. For more information see https://www.childfund.org.au/ or the Child Fund International website https://www.childfund.org/.

World Vision is another example of an organisation that supports children and their communities in developing countries. Depending on child and community needs, sponsorship projects may focus on clean water and sanitation, health and nutrition, food and agriculture, education and child rights, and income generation. You can see how child welfare is a cross cutting measure, and intersects many of the SDGs. For more information see https://sponsor.worldvision.com.au/ sponsor-a-child, or the World Vision International page https://www. worldvision.org/.

Advocating as good neighbours

Given that governments are the major donors of aid via our taxes, it seems right to become involved at a political level in order to encourage governments to be more generous. This is very much the prophetic task of the church. One of Micah Australia's current main campaigns is on Australian aid. I've already used some of their material in this chapter. At the time of writing, a new whitepaper on foreign policy is being written by the Australian government, and Micah are encouraging Christians to have their say. Given the decline in Australian aid giving, now is the time to speak up. For more information see http://www. micahaustralia.org/agency/australian_aid. Similar campaigns exist for example in the USA (http://www.micahchallengeusa.org/end_extreme_ poverty) where you can contact congressional leaders.

Each year at Voices for Justice, hundreds of like-minded Christians from all over the country descend on Canberra for prayer, worship, learning about justice issues, and speaking to politicians from a Christian framework about justice issues. If you're new to advocacy and lobbying, there is training provided. We should be thankful that we can have access to our politicians in an open democracy, so make the most of it! As former head of Micah Australia, Ben Thurley noted about Voices for Justice 2016

> For four days last week, Parliament House was transformed (yet again) by Micah Australia. For that Parliamentary Sitting Week about 70 of our nation's leaders were hearing and talking about the importance of Australia's aid program as one key way that we contribute towards building a more just, peaceful and sustainable world free from poverty.

For more information see http://www.micahaustralia.org/voicesforjustice.

Taxing like good neighbours

Governments can only give to foreign aid from their existing tax base, or else change the balance of a budget and/or raise new taxes. Governments of developing countries are able to spend more on the things people need most if they receive the tax dollars that they are owed. Most people don't like the talk of new taxes, and often changes in taxation favour the already rich. You may remember (or if you're not as old as me, have heard of) Jubilee 2000, where Christians around the world petitioned governments to drop crippling debt repayments on loans, where even the interest was hard to pay back. Cuts to essential services and cash cropping rather than feeding people meant life was hard for many due to irresponsible loans and corruption. There's not much point providing aid on the one hand, while robbing countries with the other.

As Benn Banasik, Micah Australia's Campaigns and Political Engagement Coordinator notes, tax avoidance affects those most in need in two ways.[35] Firstly, multinational corporations spread funds throughout the world to avoid tax, such that it has been conservatively estimated to rob developing nations of hundreds of billions of dollars in tax revenue. Secondly, tax avoidance undermines Australia's national revenue base, with flow on affects for the aid budget as we have already noted.

The Australian Tax Office has been given provisions to act when companies are found to be purposefully avoiding tax, but there is more that can be done. For more information see http://www.micahaustralia. org/ato_measures_against_the_tax_avoiders.

Endnotes

1 Commonwealth of Australia, *East Timor: Final Report of the Senate Foreign Affairs, Defence and Trade References Committee* (Canberra: Senate Printing Unit, Parliament House, Canberra, 2000), 130.
2 Woolcott cited in Gordon Peake, *Beloved Land: Stories, Struggles, and Secrets from Timor-Leste* (Melbourne: Scribe, 2013), 183.
3 Commonwealth of Australia, *East Timor*, 7.
4 Commonwealth of Australia, *East Timor*, 17.
5 Oxfam Australia, "You and Oxfam: Fighting poverty together," YouTube video, published 20 October, 2013.

6 Micah Australia, "Micah Australia – Australian Aid Briefing Sheet," 2016, accessed 14 February, 2017, https://d3n8a8pro7vhmx.cloudfront.net/micahaustralia/pages/755/attachments/original/1481497299/aid-briefing-sheet.pdf?1481497299.

7 Australian Council for International Development, "Understanding Aid: Explanatory paper on international and Australian aid," 3 February, 2017, accessed 3 April, 2017, http://reliefweb.int/report/world/understanding-aid-explanatory-paper-international-and-australian-aid.

8 Robin Davies, "Savage budget cuts pull Australia down in foreign aid rankings," *The Conversation*, 4 May, 2016, accessed 14 February, 2017, http://theconversation.com/savage-budget-cuts-pull-australia-down-in-foreign-aid-rankings-58854.

9 Millennium Project, "The 0.7% target: An in-depth look," *Millennium Project*, 2006, accessed 14 February, 2017, http://www.unmillenniumproject.org/press/07.htm.

10 Micah Australia, *Understanding Aid*, 14.

11 Max Bearak and Lazaro Gamio, "The U.S. foreign-aid budget, visualized," *The Washington Post*, 26 September, 2016, accessed 18 February, 2017, .https://www.washingtonpost.com/news/worldviews/wp/2016/09/26/the-u-s-foreign-aid-budget-visualized/?utm_term=.212918c5c119

12 Michael Gerson and Raj Shah, "'America first' shouldn't mean cutting foreign aid," *The Washington Post*, 24 February, 2017, accessed 25 February, 2017, https://www.washingtonpost.com/posteverything/wp/2017/02/24/america-first-shouldnt-mean-cutting-foreign-aid/?tid=hybrid_collaborative_1_na&utm_term=.52c3f540fa69.

13 Paul Karp, "Australians massively overestimate level of foreign aid in budget, poll finds," *The Guardian*, 29 April, 2016, accessed 25 February, 2017, https://www.theguardian.com/australia-news/2016/apr/29/australians-massively-overestimate-level-of-foreign-aid-in-budget-poll-finds.

14 Jonathan Pryke, "Australia's 2016 aid budget: A good start to getting off rock bottom," *The Interpreter* 5 May, 2016, accessed 25 February, 2017, https://www.lowyinstitute.org/the-interpreter/australias-2016-aid-budget-good-start-getting-rock-bottom.

15 The Hon Joe Hockey, "Press conference, Parliament House, Canberra," 15 December, 2014, accessed 25 February, 2017, http://jbh.ministers.treasury.gov.au/transcript/143-2014/.

16 Micah Australia, *Understanding Aid*, 19.

17 Gareth Hutchins, "What is the 'Buffett rule' and why does a faction of the Labor party want it?," *The Guardian*, 22 February, 2017, accessed 25 February, 2017, https://www.theguardian.com/australia-news/2017/feb/22/what-is-the-buffett-rule-and-why-does-a-faction-of-the-labor-party-want-it.

18 Karl S. Kruszelnicki, "Wound healing and air," *ABC Science,* 14 December, 2006, accessed 13 February, 2017, http://www.abc.net.au/science/articles/2006/12/14/1811582.htm.

19 Celsus, "De Medicina," W.G Spencer, Ed., Book V, Chapter 26, accessed 13 February, 2017, http://www.perseus.tufts.edu/hopper/text?doc=Cels.%205.26&lang=original.

20 Micah Australia, *Understanding Aid*, 5.

21 IPCC, 2014, *Climate Change 2014: Synthesis Report. Contribution of Working Groups I, II and III to the Fifth Assessment Report of the Intergovernmental Panel on Climate Change* [Core Writing Team, R.K. Pachauri and L.A. Meyer (eds.)]. IPCC, Geneva, Switzerland, 151 pp., 6.

22 Delphine Deryng, Declan Conway, Navin Ramankutty, Jeff Price and Rachel Warren, "Global crop yield response to extreme heat stress under multiple climate change futures," *Environmental Research Letters* 9 (2014).

23   Oxfam International, "Africa's Smallholders Adapting to Climate Change: The need for national governments and international climate finance to support women producers," 14 October, 2015, accessed 3 June, 2017, http://policy-practice.oxfam.org.uk/publications/africas-smallholders-adapting-to-climate-change-the-need-for-national-governmen-579620, 7.

24 Green Climate Fund, *Elements* 1 (November 2015), 7.

25 Oxfam International, *Africa's Smallholders Adapting to Climate Change*, 17.

26 Green Climate Fund, *Elements* 2 (November 2015), 56

27 Green Climate Fund, *Elements* 1, 10.

28 Green Climate Fund, *Elements* 2, 17.

29 Green Climate Fund, *Elements* 2, 23.

30   Annie Gowan, "India's huge need for electricity is a problem for the planet," *The Washington Post*, 6 November, 2015, accessed 25 February, 2017, https://www.washingtonpost.com/world/asia_pacific/indias-huge-need-for-electricity-is-a-problem-for-the-planet/2015/11/06/a9e004e6-622d-11e5-8475-781cc9851652_story.html?utm_term=.714d57bdb9ef.

31 Green Climate Fund, *Elements* 2, 14.

32 Emma Griffiths and Jake Sturmer, "Climate change: Julie Bishop announces Australia's $200 million contribution to UN Green Climate Fund," *ABC News*, 10 December, 2014, accessed 25 February, 2017, http://www.abc.net.au/news/2014-12-10/bishop-200-million-to-green-climate-fund-at-un-climate-summit/5956676.

33   The Hon Julia Bishop MP, "Australia to lead Green Climate Fund Board in 2017," Media Release 16 December, 2016, accessed 25 February, 2017, http://foreignminister.gov.au/releases/Pages/2016/jb_mr_161216.aspx.

34 Patrick Goodenough, "Final Days: Obama Sends $500M to UN Climate Fund; Trump Vowed to Cancel 'Global Warming Payments'," *CBS News*, 17 January, 2017, accessed 25 February, 2017, http://www.cnsnews.com/news/article/patrick-goodenough/final-days-obama-sends-another-500-million-un-climate-fund-trump-has.

35   Benn Banasik, "ATO Measures against the Tax Avoiders," *Micah Australia*, 25 February, 2016, accessed 12 March, 2017, http://www.micahaustralia.org/ato_measures_against_the_tax_avoiders.

Chapter 3 — Freedom

Modern slavery

Assam is a state in northern India. It shares its borders with six other Indian states and the neighbouring countries of Bangladesh and Bhutan. It is a region marked by ethnic tensions with Muslim migrants, and regular flooding during the wet season (July to September). To compound this, human traffickers regularly target people in the region. Take the case of Uma Tadu (not her real name).[1] At 16, floods destroyed her village. As is often the case after natural disasters, she decided to seek a better life and employment in Delhi, more than 1,600 kilometres away. Upon arrival in Delhi, Uma was sold as bonded labour. Rescued two years later, she returned to her village and a life of poverty, but became associated with Bachpan Bachao Andolan: Save the Child Unit.

Bachpan Bachao Andolan is a non-profit begun by Nobel Prize-winner Kailash Satyarthi. Satyarthi received his Nobel peace prize in 2014 along with the Pakistani teenager and women's education activist Malala Yousafzai. Over three and a half decades, he has freed tens of thousands of young Indians like Uma Tadu.[2] Four years after she was enslaved, Uma's village was attacked in December 2014 by separatist rebels during a wave of ethnic violence. More than 80,000 people were displaced at the time.[3] Sadly, the National Democratic Front of Bodoland of NDFB are Christian separatists, indigenous to the region.[4] Much of the violence tends to occur between them and Muslim Bengali migrants.[5] Thankfully after this outbreak of violence, Uma was found alive.

Both environmental disasters and ethnic tension are factors in people becoming enslaved in India. When such events happen, people traffickers like Bibek Kirki go hunting. He confided to a journalist that 'I will be going to look for girls from Sonitpur. I think I can arrange them in three to four days.'[6] Criminals like Kirki send young girls to Delhi and other cities, where they are on sold as domestic help and forced labour. Some girls like Mirila are sold to older men for marriage. As the eldest child to a single mother, the prospect of a city job seemed like a solution to their difficulties. Instead, as with so many other girls like her, it ended in forced marriage. Thankfully, Mirila was rescued after five months.

According to The Evangelical Fellowship of India Commission on Relief (EFICOR) traffickers are often known to the victims or familiar with their families. They tempt them with promise of jobs, money, a better life or marriage.[7] People are vulnerable to slavery due to poverty, in combination with a variety of factors:

- Social exclusion and alienation,
- Social exclusion as a result of the class system, gender discrimination,
- Lack of land
- Seasonal migration of male workers, leaving behind vulnerable women and girls
- Lack of access to, or value of, education
- Failure of agriculture to meet the needs of the local community throughout the year in rural trafficking hotspots
- Lack of alternatives to agricultural work in the locality
- Large-scale internal migration
- Increasing 'merchandise character' of children within a globalised free market economy
- High profit potential
- Growing tourism
- Growing national and international demand for child adoption
- Superstitious belief that sexual intercourse with very young girls (virgins) cures one from infectious diseases
- Natural catastrophes, war, or economic depression increase the danger for children to become victims of child trafficking

The slave convention of 1926 states that 'slavery is the status or condition of a person over whom any or all of the powers attaching to the right of ownership are exercised.' In 1948, article 4 of the Universal Convention of Human Rights declared that 'No one shall be held in slavery or servitude; slavery and the slave trade shall be prohibited in all their forms.'[8] This is a declaration to aspire to, but sadly there is still a long way to go. India is in the Tier II list of countries in the UN, which consists of countries that have failed to combat human trafficking.[9] As you can see, the causes of slavery really are quite complex. This chapter will examine the issue of slavery, looking at the specific circumstances where climate change leads to people ending up being trafficked.

A (very) brief history of slavery[10]

The word slave comes from Slav, referring to Slavonic people who were enslaved in Europe in great numbers from the 6th to 10th centuries. According to International Justice Mission, 45 million people were in slavery and forced labour in 2016. Slavery generates more than $190 billion per year.[11] Compare this to the Atlantic slave trade. From about 1500 to 1870, about 10 million slaves were taken from Africa to the Americas.[12] That's right, there are more slaves globally now than in the Americas during the Atlantic slave trade! Slavery has been with us a long time. The ancient Greek states permitted slavery, and during the classical period of Athens, from the fifth to third centuries BCE, one third of the population were slaves. The Roman Empire lived off the back of slaves, something we will talk more about below. Slavery has also existed in Islamic countries, and there is no condemnation of slavery in either the Qur'an or Hadith. Of course, the Old Testament is also ambiguous on slavery.

As mentioned earlier, the Atlantic trade moved about 10 million people during 370 years. African slavers preferred to take women and boys, usually killing the men. The Atlantic trade ironically saved many from death, bound for plantations to grow sugar, coffee, and cotton, to work in mines, or as domestic servants. One bright spot of course was William Wilberforce and the Clapham Sect, who worked to abolish the slave trade in the British Empire in 1807, and then slavery altogether in 1833. It should be noted that this was no overnight success. For example, after Wilberforce made an impassioned speech on 18 April 1791, where he gave accounts of murder, rape, torture, and the impacts of slavery on Africa, the vote for abolition was rejected by 163 votes to 88.[13] This should highlight both that whatever is legal is not necessarily moral, and whatever is immoral and yet legal, can take a long time to change.

Of course, Christianity has had an ambiguous history with regards to slavery. As Larry Morrison points out, Christians in the Southern United States defended slavery based upon a literal reading of Scripture.[14] Stories like the cursing of Ham by Noah were taken as divine approval of slavery, which could be applied to American slave ownership. The fulfilment of the prophecy was said to apply not just to Ham, but all of his descendants. There was, according to such a view, no rescinding of the permission to own slaves.[15] Furthermore, texts like Leviticus 25:44-46 were taken as divine ordination of slavery for all time. In a typically Fundamentalist 'house of cards' approach to Scripture, a newspaper correspondent referred to this passage and insisted that it had to be believed or else we 'flatly deny the whole of the bible.'[16] I'm going to pike out on a treatment of slavery in the Old Testament, and move instead to the New Testament. After all, it is through Jesus that we are to understand and apply the Old Testament, and that is where generations of Christians have gone wrong on this issue.

Status quo or quietly subversive

When we read the New Testament texts on slavery, we have to understand the role that slavery played in the Roman Empire. Rome was built upon a patriarchal structure, the *paterfamilias*, with Caesar as father supreme. The economic order relied on the control of women, children and slaves. Even freed slaves continued to be under their master's power as part of a patron-client relationship, with those patrons themselves being clients to others, all the way up to Caesar. Such a relationship was manipulative, promising resources to the client but never fully delivering.[17] Clients were expected to vote for patrons when they were running for public office, and ransom them if they were taken prisoner. Slavery in a real sense was for life. As Tom Wright notes, slavery in the ancient world (as it is now) was a great evil, from which many profited. Slaves had no rights, were open to all sorts of abuse, and could be subject to torture or death for trivial offenses.[18]

On the face of it, Paul would appear to be only interested in maintaining the status quo of empire. In 1 Corinthians 7:21, he tells Christian slaves not to be concerned by their status. In Colossians 3:22-4:1 and Ephesians 6:5-9, he has commands for Christian slaves and their masters! Then there is the curious passage in Galatians 3:28-29. In Christ, no distinctions matters, be it male and female, Jew or Gentile, slave or free. Does that mean Paul thinks it simply doesn't matter who you are or what situation you find yourself in? Do we have to go outside of the New Testament for support for an anti-slavery cause? Not at all, it just might not be what we'd hope for, but hold on to your presuppositions for now.

Paul's letter to Philemon holds the key, but you have to read carefully. The letter is addressed to Philemon on the occasion of his slave Onesimus having run away. While some older commentators argue Philemon was not the owner, it makes most sense of the letter that he is. Nothing hangs on it for our purposes. Paul writes not only to Philemon about this matter, but to the whole of his household and the church gathering that meets there. What is to follow is a corporate matter, for corporate reconciliation. Paul writes with the confidence that this is a loving Christian community, who love Christ and the saints (verses 4-7). So while he can pull rank as an apostle, he much prefers to appeal to their love as Christians (verses 8-9). Here we should once more be reminded of the dual call to love God and neighbour from our favourite parable.

So what is Paul's request? As Wright points out, in the first place it isn't for Onesimus to be released from slavery, as much as we would like it to be so. We need to be patient before we get to that! The first goal is reconciliation. Onesimus may have left Colossae and the house of Philemon as a runaway slave, but now he is their brother, i.e. a fellow Christian (verse 16) and this is how Paul expects Philemon to accept Onesimus. Wright argues that this is not a request for emancipation, but a definite change in the relationship to reflect the various passages about slave-master relationships. Onesimus' change in status is described in his new father-son relationship to Paul (verse 10) and now how he has gone from being useless (was he an indolent slave?) to useful to them and Paul. The name Onesimus literally means profitable or useful. Philemon and his household should welcome Onesimus as they would welcome Paul (verse 17). Paul again reminds them of what they owe him as an apostle, but that if Onesimus owes Philemon anything, Paul will repay the debt (verses 18-19). Perhaps he ran away with some of his master's money. Regardless, Philemon is to forgive and they are all to be reconciled.

So are there hints of release? Certainly verse 16 and the new filial relationship forms a framework where emancipation may occur. Paul asks for, but does not demand, a form of emancipation. He wants to keep Onesimus with him in the service of the gospel (verse 13), and has already described their close relationship and his value to Paul (verses 10-11). If they sent Onesimus back to Paul, he could effectively no longer be Philemon's slave, or at the very least while he is legally his slave, he acts as his representative, aiding Paul in the gospel. Philemon has already been described as a co-worker with Paul (verse 2), and now Onesimus is as well. Why shouldn't this continue while Paul is in chains in Rome? The letter is all hints and teasing. We'd love a clear answer, but don't get one. The last hint is in verses 20-22. Philemon owes Paul much, but Paul will pay any debt Onesimus has incurred. But Paul still wants to visit Philemon and gain some benefit from him. The word in Greek for benefit is related to the name Onesimus, again a subtle hint! Furthermore, confident in Philemon's obedience, Paul believes that 'you will do even more than I say (NRSV).' Surely when Paul visits he is hopeful for emancipation for Onesimus.

So why is it all cloak and dagger here? And is there a difference between then and now? Onesimus could certainly have been legally beaten for what he had done, something that was normal and acceptable.[19] Wright seems to think that it was a matter of timing. Paul was jailed for proclaiming another king (Acts 17:7), and certainly viewed the new age as having arrived. But being too loud about emancipation in the setting in which he found himself would have made life more difficult for slaves. Paul did not want to encourage an uprising, because they had happened before, were usually violent, and never ended well. He would not want to even give the hint that he might support such a thing. Wright also thinks that even if Christians released their slaves, this would not have been effective in changing the social order of the day. It would certainly have been controversial. So Paul had to walk a fine line to not be seen as advocating insurrection, as indeed we need to do today.

What Paul does is far more subtle. In 1 Corinthians the priority is being a slave of Christ, which is real freedom (1 Corinthians 7:21-23). That said, verse 21 suggests that seeking freedom is a good thing to do. However, while slavery as an institution existed in Roman society, it could be redefined. Slaves could be brothers and sisters to their masters, and vice versa, instead of mere property as under Roman law. Furthermore, slaves serve their heavenly master in serving their earthly master, and masters care for their slaves because they too have a master in heaven (Colossians 3:22-4:1). This might seem far less than we would like, but in its context, it was revolutionary. As Walsh and Keesmaat point out, Paul uses the language of inheritance when he writes in verse 24 'you will receive the inheritance as your reward.'[20] The language of inheritance places slaves at the centre of the great story of Israel post exile. I discuss this idea as it appears in Ezekiel 47:13-14 in more detail in the chapter on refugees. For now, we need to understand that Paul writes to Colossae with the full biblical narrative in mind, one that Philemon should therefore have known when Paul wrote his short letter to him. This is the gospel that means that the Jubilee year has arrived, and that slaves are to be freed (Luke 4:18-19).

In our age though, there is no need to be quite so tentative. Not concerned about the power of Rome, we live in a society shaped in the past by the gospel, and an understanding that it is not good for one person to own another. We are not a persecuted minority as the church was when Paul was writing. What he could only hint at, we can discuss explicitly. We have the Universal Declaration, but we also have the gospel. Christians have for many years combated the evil of slavery. In the 21st century, in order to understand the dynamics of slavery in many contexts, we must also understand climate change. And so it is to that connection we now turn.

The climate connection

Now let's return to India. Assam and the whole of northeast India is described as very fragile and an environmentally sensitive zone, with increasing temperatures and declining rainfall, threatening peoples' livelihoods.[21] It shouldn't be surprising that there is a climate change connection to flooding. River flows in India are driven by local rainfall and upstream glaciers in the Himalayas. Rivers can break their banks due to very heavy rainfall associated with the monsoon. Climate change is affecting the monsoonal rainfall, resulting in more variable rainfall. Yearly rainfall totals are declining, while individual rain events can be very heavy. Climate change is also producing more river flow as rising temperatures in the Himalayas cause the melting of snow and ice. In this section, we will look at two Indian states and how climate change is affecting flooding.

In 2015, Daniel Grossman wrote an article for the website Yale Environment 360 which examined the causes of the 2013 flood of the Mandakini River in the Indian state of Uttarakhand.[22] The flood occurred on June 17, and was India's worst disaster in a decade, with several thousand drowning deaths, and loss of livestock and infrastructure. There were complex factors involved, including poorly built homes, unregulated development, and soil erosion caused by Hindu pilgrims. However, climate change played a major role.

Rainfall had been in steady decline in the state during the period 1950 to 2010, and the monsoon has become more irregular.[23] However, monsoonal rainfall in the two weeks before the flood was unprecedented; twice as much rainfall fell in the first two weeks of June than the same period over the prior 60 years. On the 16th of June, the day before the flood, some 330 mm was measured at Chorabari Tal, a glacial lake at the head of Chorabari Glacier. This is likely an underestimate as the rain gauge was washed away during the flooding. Glacial lakes are like Chorabari Tal formed by glacial melting, and are typically surrounded by moraines, masses of rocks and sediment carried down and deposited by the glacier. Chorabari Tal fills seasonally, and then the porous moraine allows water to drain out, lowering the water level. In the

June flood, the moraine ruptured catastrophically, releasing nearly 400 million litres of water.

Deepti Singh and co-authors found that the heavy rainfall that produced the flood resulted from what they described as an anomalously early arrival of a monsoon-like atmospheric circulation over India.[24] In less technical terms, the rainy season came early and it came in spades. The resulting rainfall was in the top 20% of totals for June over much of central and northern India. Monsoon onset occurs when there is a reversal of the temperature gradient between the continent and the oceans through a large depth of the atmosphere. This reversal produces deep westerly winds, bringing warm and moisture-laden air off the oceans onto the land. The air temperatures over land were very high, resulting in an early reversal of the winds. Likewise, the air blowing over India was very humid. This too is consistent with global warming, as warmer air temperatures evaporate more moisture from the oceans. The more moisture the air holds, the more rainfall can condense in heavy downpours. Finally, it turns out that the weather pattern in the upper atmosphere was also unusual for the time of year, further adding to the mix.

Singh and co-authors then tested the hypothesis as to whether or not climate change was playing a role in the flood. Heavy early rains due to warm, moist conditions are certainly consistent with this idea. They examined runs of climate models using both 20th century and pre-industrial period values of carbon dioxide in the atmosphere. Singh and co-authors found that of the 11 climate models they examined, 7 showed an increased likelihood of a severe flooding event compared to the pre-industrial period. Further, they were able to show that it is just as likely as not that we have tipped the balance of the atmosphere, so that heavy rainfall during June in India is twice as likely to happen now as without our interference with the climate. The other factor in the flood was melting glaciers, which feed the Mandakini River. A study conducted for conditions in Nepal found that melting Himalayan glaciers change the dynamics of rivers fed by them, and lead to glacial lakes that grow rapidly and are at increased risk of bursting and flooding.[25] Such was the case for Chorabari Tal.

57

The story we began with looked at conditions in the Indian state of Assam. Debojyoti Das examined the impacts of flooding on a tribal community in Majuli, the largest river island of the Brahmaputra River basin in Assam.[26] The 2011 population of the island was 168,000 people. About 21% of these people live below the poverty line of $2 per day. The island is vulnerable to flooding from the river and erosion of the river banks. As a result, the area of Majuli has been slowly shrinking. Erosion is a major problem since over 90% of people on the island are dependent on agriculture for their livelihood. Flash flooding from heavy rains is also a significant problem. As we have discussed previously, climate change can lead to a more variable monsoon with heavy rains.

Floods impact the lives of the people of Majuli as they destroy crops, houses, and wash away cattle. Damage to crop lands can be irreversible due to heavy silt deposits and salt deposition. Since rainwater is the source of water for irrigation, variable monsoon rainfall impacts water availability, and crop yields have decreased over time with decreasing rainfall. The overall impact has been a 30% decrease in household earnings over a decade. Literacy rates are high at over 70% for the island, but the number of people with higher education remains low, making alternative employment more difficult to obtain. Migration is an option, as men move to other districts to obtain jobs as semi-skilled workers in factories and as security guards, while the women tend to stay behind to care for children and the elderly. Migration means money can be sent home to service debt, and is a way of avoiding falling into bonded labour. However, it has been reported that much of the work is low-skilled, precarious, and dangerous.[27] Women who migrate are vulnerable to ending up in brothels.[28] Further, a declining local workforce is bad for the local economy, and increases the work burden of the women left behind. It also increases the susceptibility to trafficking of those left behind.[29]

A global issue

To sum up then, there is a close link in northern India (and indeed in many other parts) between climate change, poverty (which in itself is an injustice), and human trafficking. But it's not just an issue in India. In Kenya, a lack of adequate education, extreme poverty and climate change are creating conditions where Maasai parents are unknowingly giving up their children to traffickers.[30] This is a phenomenon not only in Kenya, but in parts of West and Central Africa. Families in poverty send their children away in the hope that they might make their fortune in big cities or overseas. Instead, while some girls end up in prostitution, most children are sold into some form of bonded labour. The deception in this by trafficking agents needs to be stressed. No one 'sells' their children knowingly into slavery.[31]

Traffickers enter the Maasai region posing as tourists, and stay in lodges in the townships. Climate change makes it harder for families to get enough food for everyone, as their goats and cattle die. Drought over the past few years has been producing economic refugees. A drought in 2014 was followed by poor rains in 2015 and 2016, with poor conditions during March to May of 2017 as well. It has been described as the worst drought for over 70 years. In 2016, the wet season rain during the period March to May was poor, leaving 1.3 million Kenyans in need of food aid.[32] Water levels are dropping in rivers, due to declining rainfall and expanding agriculture.[33]

The Maasai are often forced to sell their land cheaply as a result of the changing climate, leaving them without an economic base in an effective repeat of what happened during the colonial period.[34] Other pressures on land include rapid urbanisation and the purchase of land by the Kenyan middle class, and pressures from tourism. All along the way, corruption abounds as local authorities conspire with developers to privatise land.[35] Big money can be involved, and there is demand for hunting by tourists from the United Arab Emirates leading to expanding park boundaries and hence contracting areas for cattle herding.[36]

Maasai girls, as girls everywhere, are particularly vulnerable to trafficking. Economic pressures mean that the Maasai seek to marry girls off earlier in order to gain access to dowries to feed their families. Typically in Maasai culture, girls are promised in marriage as babies, or even before birth.[37] The difference here between arranged marriages and opportunistic human traffickers is that the girls are never heard from again. Maasai girls miss out on an education, as families often cannot afford the education costs. There is also an issue of safety, given the distances that girls have to travel to go to school. Since 1999, Children's Fund have run a program to prevent child marriages by promising girls to school rather than to a husband, and giving gifts instead of a dowry to the father. As in India, women suffer disproportionately under the impacts of climate change. SDG 5 is the goal of achieving gender equality. As we have seen, climate change makes this goal more difficult to achieve.

Campaigning against slavery

I first became aware of modern slavery watching the documentary *Born into Brothels*.[38] The film highlights the plight of children born into brothels in Calcutta, and the risks especially for girls who can't receive an education. The film was criticised by various groups for falling into racist stereotypes, and being a piece of Indophobic propaganda. Since then, however, the charity *Kids with Cameras* who were responsible for the film have partnered with Head First Development in building Hope House, a safe house for young girls. The Hope House website has this to say about the project:

> Girls born into Calcutta's red-light district are at extreme risk for being forced into prostitution. Even for those who are not made to sell their body, the chances of making a life for themselves outside the dangerous neighborhood are slim. The Hope House (currently under construction) will be a safe, productive, and fun residence where parents can volunteer to have their daughters live and achieve a bright and healthy future. The Hope House is located one hour away from downtown Calcutta on a beautiful property with mango trees, open fields, and an active pond – close enough that parents can still play an active role in their daughter's life, but safely distanced from the risks of their home neighborhood.
>
> For more information see http://headfirstdevelopment.org/hope/.

My other introduction to modern slavery was through a talk by David Batstone, self-described Bruce Willis lookalike, and head of *Not For Sale*. Not for Sale describes itself as 'A network to grow self-sustaining social projects with purpose-driven business to end exploitation and forced labor.' The organisation has projects in places like Peru, Thailand, and Amsterdam, where it has 'fed, housed, and educated hundreds of thousands of people affected by human trafficking and forced labor.'

Furthermore, it has started a heath drink REBBL, where the ingredients have been sourced to support those in forced labour in Peru.

This business process has been repeated in Thailand and Amsterdam. The model supports the idea we have seen before, not simply of providing for immediate needs like food, shelter, and medical care, but also 'the personal growth of the people we serve — so that they can independently support themselves and lead others through similar struggles.' Remember, *mishpat* is about allowing people to flourish on their own, not remain as dependents (except of course to God).

For more information see https://www.notforsalecampaign.org/.

TEAR Australia partner with the Evangelical Fellowship of India Commission on Relief (EFICOR). EFICOR began as part of the Evangelical Fellowship of India (EFI) in 1967, when a drought in the state of Bihar resulted in severe famine. Since then, EFICOR has instituted programs for people with HIV/AIDS, people with disabilities, climate change, disaster response, urban poverty, health, and livelihoods. As we have seen, bonded labour or slavery cuts across a number of these areas. For example, urban poverty projects focus on childcare, nutrition and school enrolments, where special emphasis is placed on girls, who can be at risk of being forced into marriages or prostitution.

Employment is essential to avoiding poverty and enslavement. Twenty year old Anjali is speech and hearing impaired. Through EFICOR's Livelihood Resource Centre, she and her husband received training, counselling, and learned job skills. Both now work at the Lemon Tree Hotel in Gurgaon. Anjali says 'RC's support has changed our lives. How can they work having a disability – people asked. What was impossible became possible because of LRC. A very special thanks to LRC!'

You can support EFICOR via http://www.tear.org.au or at http://www.eficor.org.

One major factor in global slavery is the failure of justice systems at various levels. What happens to the poor if governments have limited law enforcement resources? Or what if police officers have been given little training in criminal investigation or evidence collection? Or what if law enforcement agencies are not held accountable? What is there to stop corruption? I asked Andrew Starr of International Justice Mission (IJM) in Australia to talk about their work.

What if the Jericho road had been well policed?

'The story Jesus tells in Luke 10 of the man assaulted on his way from Jerusalem to Jericho is a familiar one: the violence and humiliation of the attack, the hypocritical busyness of the priest and the Levite, the startlingly subversive Samaritan protagonist. The timelessness of the story is haunting.

If we are honest, we can recognise ourselves in the thieves as we exert what power we have to exploit those weaker than we are. And we find ourselves too in the man bloodied and torn. Road-sided. We see that Christ has come just as the Samaritan to our aid.

The text has inspired and informed millennia of Christian engagement with the suffering. We must see, we must stop, we must care.

Imagine—despite the historical improbability—the journey of this traveller from Jerusalem if that road had been effectively policed?

At International Justice Mission this possibility is our preoccupation. IJM has been working for the past 20 years across the developing world. We are Christian lawyers, investigators, social workers, community activists and other professionals. Over these years we have met tens of thousands of people for whom the Jericho road experience of violence is a reality they have all too regularly endured.

Violence in the developing world is endemic. When we refer to violence, we mean everyday violence, not wars or genocide but everyday criminal acts: rape, child abuse, police brutality, trafficking, slavery.

At IJM our goal is simple: to protect the poor from that violence.

This chapter is of course focused on the issue of slavery. Slavery today is vast and brutal as you will have read.

Slavery today is also marked by an important conundrum. For the first time in history slavery is illegal in nearly every country, yet it exists almost everywhere. Why?

After 20 years of working on the frontlines of this fight, it is our observation that one of the main reasons that slavery and other forms of violence against the poor flourishes is quite simple: the perpetrators of that violence are not getting into trouble for it.

Slave owners and traffickers—those who prey upon the world's vulnerable poor—are not brave. They are business people. Their business thrives in an environment where the laws that exist to prohibit their violent exploitation of others are not enforced. But when we disrupt their business model, the violence stops. We have seen this demonstrated time and again in our work combating trafficking in Southeast Asia. There, in the last decade, we have seen the number of minors being trafficked into the commercial sex trade drop by between 65 and 86 percent in six different metropolitan centres.

The efficacy of this approach should and does embolden us.

Yet every iceberg has a tip. We are deeply aware that slavery is but one horrific manifestation of violence against the poor. Violence against the poor affects billions. Indeed the UN estimates that 4 billion people live outside the protection of the law. If they were to call the equivalent of '000', no one would come. No one would heed their cry or come to their protection.

This absence of effective law enforcement is lethal. It decimates our best efforts at sustainable, holistic development. An example is a girl's capacity to go to school. We know that educating girls is vital. Yet if violence is unchecked in the girl's community, studies show, she will stop going to school.

The good news is that when public justice systems actually begin to work, when the good laws prohibiting trafficking and other violent crimes are enforced, the violence drops dramatically.

This work of transforming justice systems is slow, hard and vital. What we've learned is that it happens through partnerships. The first step—as the story of the Good Samaritan teaches us—is to remove the victim of violence from harm. Since we began, in partnership with local authorities, we have relieved more than 34,000 people from oppression. But rescue alone is of course insufficient, so in partnership, our social workers are providing holistic aftercare for thousands of survivors of violent injustice.

To stop the violence from continuing, it is vital that the arm of the perpetrator is restrained. This is no simple task. In the countries with the most slaves, you are more likely to be struck by lightning than to go to jail for your crimes. Yet convictions are occurring more frequently. Globally, since we began, we have seen more than 1,200 convictions.

Finally, we work to make the Jericho road safe. We work to make the streets, the courtyards, and the factories of our global village places where children, men and women can walk and work without fear. Case by case we are seeing this change realised. With local authorities, we identify the blockages and weaknesses of the justice system and then we bring repair. To that end, since 2012, we have trained more than 46,000 officers and officials.

Amartya Sen reminds us: 'freedom from crime and violence are key components of development. Freedom from fear is as important as freedom from want. It is impossible to truly enjoy one of these rights without the other.'

God is at work setting his world right. Integral to that is policing the road, so that the flourishing God made us for can occur. We know this is possible. We know it works. The challenge now is to effect this change on a scale where billions of our neighbours are protected. Join us at IJM.org.au.'

Endnotes

1 Priyali Sur, "Conflict and Climate Change Collide in Assam as Trafficking Thrives," *New Security Beat*, 17 February, 2015, accessed 4 March, 2017, https://www.newsecuritybeat. org/2015/02/conflict-climate-change-collide-assam-girls-pushed-slavery/.

2 Jason Burke, "Who is Nobel peace prize winner Kailash Satyarthi?" *The Guardian*, 11 October, 2014, accessed 4 March, 2017, https://www.theguardian.com/world/2014/oct/10/ nobel-peace-prize-winner-kailash-satyarthi.

3 Samudra Gupta Kashyap, "Over 75,000 take shelter in relief camps in Kokrajhar; Army goes all-out against Bodo rebels in Assam," *The Indian Express*, 27 December, 2014, accessed 4 March, 2017, http://indianexpress.com/article/india/india-others/over-75000-take-shelter-in-relief-camps-in-kokrajhar-army-goes-all-out-against-rebels/.

4 Titu Shadowson, "Christian terrorist group massacres 75 civilians in Assam," *Sanskrit Magazine*, 26 December, 2014, accessed 4 March, 2017, http://www.sanskritimagazine. com/newsworthy/christian-terrorist-group-massacres-75-civilians-assam/.

5 Subir Bhaumik, "What lies behind Assam violence?" *BBC News*, 26 July, 2012, accessed 4 March, 2017, http://www.bbc.com/news/world-asia-india-18993905.

6 Priyali Sur, *Conflict and Climate Change Collide in Assam.*

7 Anita Kanaiya, "Human Trafficking - A Modern Day Slavery?" *Drishtikone* Issue 3 (2012): 3-5.

8 Baroness Caroline Cox, and Dr John Marks, *This Immoral Trade: Slave in the 21ˢᵗ Century* (Oxford: Monarch Books, 2006), 117.

9 Drishtikone Editorial Team, "Human Trafficking: The facts," *Drishtikone* Issue 3 (2012), 13.

10 The brief history is taken from Cox, and Marks, *This Immoral Trade*, chapter 4.

11 International Justice Mission Australia website, accessed 4 March, 2017, https://give.ijm.org.au/.

12 Cox, and Marks, *This Immoral Trade*, 124.

13 Stephen Tomkins, *The Clapham Sect: How Wilberforce's Circle Transformed Britain* (Oxford: Lion Hudson, 2010): 89-90.

14 Larry R. Morrison, "The Religious Defence of American Slavery Before 1830," *The Journal of Religious Thought* 37:2 (1980): 16-29.

15 Morrison, *Religious Defence of American Slavery*, 18.

16 Morrison, *Religious Defence of American Slavery*, 19.

17 Brian J. Walsh, and Sylvia C. Keesmaat, *Colossians Remixed: Subverting the Empire* (Downers Grove: Intervarsity Press, 2004): 59.

18 N. T. Wright, *The Epistles of Paul to the Colossians and to Philemon* (Leicester: Inter-Varsity Press, 1999): 169.

19 Bradley, K. R., *Slavery and Rebellion in the Roman World* (Bloomington: Indiana University Press, 1989): 129.

20 Walsh, and Keesmaat, *Colossians Remixed,* 207.

21 Amarjyoti Borah, Sabita Devi, and Manisha Medhi, *Impact of Climate Change on Marginalised Women: An Exploratory study across 6 districts in Assam* (INECC, 2012): 8.

22 Daniel Grossman, "Unnatural Disaster: How Climate Helped Cause India's Big Flood," *Yale Environment 360* 23 June, 2015, accessed 6 February, 2017, http://e360.yale.edu/features/unnatural_disaster_how_global_warming_helped_cause_indias_catastrophic_flood.

23 Borah, Devi, and Medhi, *Impact of Climate Change*, 9.

24 Deepti Singh, et. al., "Severe Precipitation in Northern India in June 2013: Causes, Historical Context, and Changes in Probability," *Bulletin of the American Meteorological Society* 95:4 (2015): 558-561.

25 Arun B. Shresstha and Raju Aryal, "Climate Change in Nepal and its Impact on Himalayan Glaciers," *Regional Environmental Change* 11 (2011): S65-S77.

26 Debojyoti Das, "Changing climate and its impacts on Assam, Northeast India," *Bandung: Journal of the Global South* 2:26 (2015). DOI 10.1186/s40728-015-0028-4.

27 Nicole Molinari, "Intensifying Insecurities: The impact of climate change on vulnerability to human trafficking in the Indian Sundarbans," *Anti Trafficking Review* 8 (2017), 8.

28 Manipadma Jena, "Women bear the brunt of climate-forced migration," *India Climate Dialogue*, 4 January, 2017, accessed 3 June, 2017, http://indiaclimatedialogue.net/2017/01/04/women-bear-brunt-climate-forced-migration/.

29 Molinari, *Intensifying Insecurities*, 6-8.
30 Charles Njeru, "KENYA: Climate Change, Poverty and Tourists put Maasai Daughters at Risk," *Women News Network*, 16 April, 2010, accessed 4 March, 2017, https://womennewsnetwork.net/2010/04/16/kenya-climatechange-trafficking-892/.
31 Mike Dottridge, "Trafficking in children in West and Central Africa," *Gender & Development*, 10 (2002): 38-42.
32 Katy Migiro, "Drought to intensify in Kenya in 2017, new early warning system shows," *Reuters*, 13 December, 2016, accessed 4 March, 2017, http://www.reuters.com/article/us-kenya-drought-idUSKBN1421WH.
33 Patricia Kameri-Mboti, and Elvin Nyukuri, "Climate change, law, and indigenous people in Kenya," in Abate Randall S. and Elizabeth Ann Kronk, eds, *Climate Change, Indigenous Peoples and the Search for Legal Remedies* (London: Edward Elgar, 2014): 9.
34 Charles Njeru, *Kenya*.
35 Shadrack Kavilu, "Kenya's rapid urbanisation takes toll on Maasai communal land," *Reuters*, 31 July, 2016, accessed 9 March, 2017, http://www.reuters.com/article/kenya-landrights-maasai-idUSL8N1A728G.
36 Jason Patinkin, "Maasai fury as plan to lure Arabian Gulf tourists threatens their ancestral land," *The Guardian*, 32? March 2013, accessed 9 March, 2017, https://www.theguardian.com/world/2013/mar/30/maasai-game-hunting-tanzania.
37 Andrea Parrot, and Nina Cummings, *Sexual Enslavement of Girls and Women Worldwide* (Westport, CT: Greenwood Publishing Group, 2008): 84.
38 Zana Briski, *Born into Brothels: Calcutta's Red Light Kids*. DVD. Directed by Zana Briski, and Ross Kauffman. New York: Redlight Films, 2004.

Chapter 4 — Fortress western world

The child who changed the narrative

Syria has been in the news all too often for all the wrong reasons. Civil war has been going on since 2011 between forces loyal to the president Bashar al-Assad and anti-government protestors. Add to that jihadist militants from the so-called Islamic State (ISIS), and you have a bloody conflict. Islamic sectarianism also plays a role between the president's Shia sect and the Sunni majority. The politics is further complicated by Kurds to the north, and foreign involvement, from Russian and Iranian involvement propping up the government, to that of the US led coalition. The conflict is ugly, and has included the use of chemical weapons, allegedly by not just government forces, but also by ISIS.

In March of 2016, the number of refugees to have fled Syria exceeded 4.5 million, with an estimated further 6.5 million people internally displaced. The UN estimated that over $3 billion was required to provide for the humanitarian needs during 2016. Many of those internally displaced have been beyond humanitarian aid due to the unwillingness of the warring parties to provide safe passage to aid workers. To date, the vast majority of refugees have relocated to Turkey, Lebanon, and Jordan.[1] Some have made it to Europe, although by no means not all successfully. One of the problems with refugees is that it is very easy to see them as a faceless mass of humanity, and this sometimes is used to depersonalise, dehumanise, demonise, or scapegoat them. The opposite risk when writing about refugees and their plight is to focus on the story of one individual and make them into a project, rather than a person, as Eugene Cho might say. We take from their humanity rather than add to it. Yet stories can also be valuable, even though they may be sad ones.

This brings us to the haunting images of three year old Alan Kurdi. Alan and his brother came from the northern Syrian town of Kobani, where fighting between Kurds and Islamic insurgents has been particularly fierce. Alan was one of 12 Syrians who drowned attempting to reach the Greek island of Kos in two boats. This young boy's body was washed up on a beach not far from the resort town of Bodrum, dressed in a bright red t-shirt and shorts. A second image of a Turkish policeman gingerly carrying the boy's body away from the beach went viral on the social media site Twitter. Alan Kurdi's fate is a grim reminder of the desperation of those fleeing the Syrian violence. Some 2,500 people also arrived on the Greek island of Lesbos that day, in similarly unseaworthy vessels.[2] It shouldn't take this sort of story to attract our attention to such a humanitarian crisis, but often it sharpens our focus. Looking at the images of Alan's body on the beach, I think of when my son was three years old. His main interests included Thomas the Tank Engine and Bob the Builder, not fleeing oppression.

Of course, such tragic images are not always treated as they deserve to be, as the 2001 'Tampa incident' demonstrates. In August of 2001, the Norwegian freighter Tampa rescued 438 Afghan asylum seekers. The Australian Government released photographs purportedly showing children who had been thrown overboard by their parents, allegedly to gain sympathy for their plight and find easy access into Australia. No such thing occurred. The former head of publicity of the Defence Department has since said that she was told there was 'to be nothing in the public forum which would humanise these people. We were quite stunned.'[3] Images can control how people respond to others in need, but they are not always enough, particularly when they are put in the hands of spin doctors.

Closing doors, closing hearts

The response to the inflow of refugees from Syria into Europe has been mixed.[4] Some European countries have been generous in the past in terms of the numbers of refugees that they have accepted. In 2015, Germany suspended the 'Dublin regulation' that required that refugees must seek asylum in the first EU country they reach. This was unfair to countries like Greece and Italy, which is often the first port of call for those fleeing Syria. France, Italy and the Netherlands have also been generous. But there have been countries that have not been so helpful. The UK has fairly high immigration rates, but in 2015 David Cameron set a target of settling 20,000 refugees by 2020. However, a

2016 report suggested Britain is nowhere near being on track to reach this target.[5] Some countries have a closed door mentality, such as those who were formerly under Soviet rule. Slovakia is only willing to take a few hundred Christians as opposed to Muslims, while Hungary and the Czech Republic have spoken in the past about using armed forces to protect their borders.[6]

Regardless of official policy, the crisis has raised concerns with citizens, leading to a rise in the profile of far right politics. In May of 2016, Austria came within a few hundred votes of electing a far-right president, Norbert Hofer of Austria's Freedom Party. The Freedom Party was founded by former Nazi SS officers. The day after the election, the government announced it would make its immigration laws more in line with those of Hofer's party. Austria formerly adopted an approach more like Germany's, but then closed its borders in reaction to public concern.[7] Given recent rhetoric of 'America First' in US politics, it is interesting to note that the motto of Austria's far right party is 'Austria first.'[8] In January of 2016, a similar phenomenon was observed in Norway, where the ruling Liberal party introduced new immigration laws. So even when the far right does not get elected, it still drives the agenda on issues like immigration.[9] Given that the Syrian crisis is one of the drivers of this shift to the right, it is unsurprising that the Greek far right group Golden Dawn are campaigning against the 'Islamisation of Greece.'[10]

In the US, Amanda Marcotte argues that Trump has imported this European style of far right ideology.[11] Her argument is that while talk of a wall at the US-Mexico border is nothing new, the level of discussion about Syria is new and out of place. Trump scapegoated Mexicans as rapists in order to muster support for his wall, and in the southern states in particular support has not been lacking. However, as Marcotte points out, in August of 2016 when Trump first mentioned Syria, only 8,000 Syrian refugees had been settled in the US. The total number of Muslim refugees to enter the US in 2016 was about 0.01% of the US population. So why should Republicans make such a big deal over what appears to be such a small issue? For Marcotte, this is a signal from Trump to the far right in Europe that he is on their side. Trump pointedly castigated

Angela Merkel's policy when he said 'I think that Europe has made a tremendous mistake by allowing these millions of people to go into Germany and various other countries. And all you have to do is take a look. It's a disaster what's happening over there.' Trumps attitude is mirrored by Donald Trump Jr. who compared Syrian refugees to poisoned skittles.[12]

It is easy enough to point the finger at other nations, but it does show how widespread the attitude of suspicion, if not downright hostility, to asylum seekers and refugees is. On a 2016 visit to Australia, Naomi Klein pointed out that while the US wanted to build a wall, Australia already had one; 'I think we shouldn't be so self-satisfied about it. You're actually doing it, he's just talking about it.' She described the conditions in the detention centres on Nauru and Manus Island as an 'international atrocity,' as well as decrying the silencing of whistle blowers.[13]

There has now been over 15 years of offshore processing of asylum claims.[14] Offshore detention restarted in 2001, and has been carried out by both Labor and Coalition governments. This restart of an internationally condemned policy followed the Tampa incident discussed earlier, when Australia refused the Norwegian freighter entry into Australian waters. John Howard's 'Pacific solution' meant that asylum seekers would have their cases processed on Nauru, and Manus Island off mainland Papua New Guinea. The Coalition removed Christmas Island from the Australian migration zone, and 10 years later a Labor government removed the entire Australian mainland. The Howard government was re-elected with the cry of 'we will decide who comes to this country and the manner in which they come.'[15] The arrival of boats slowed, and by 2008 offshore processing was ended under the Rudd Labor government. Two high profile disasters at sea contributed to a death toll of more than 1000, leading to the 'Malaysian solution' under Julia Gillard's Labor government in 2011. This deal, for Malaysia to take asylum seekers from Australia, was struck down by the high court. A similar deal with Cambodia under coalition immigration minister Scott Morrison was also unsuccessful, with only six people having been resettled.

Conditions in detention have led to serious physical and mental health issues. The list of abuses is truly horrifying. Widespread sexual and physical abuse has been reported, including over 1000 incidents involving children, as recorded in the Nauru files.[16] Cases include the slapping of children, death threats, and the giving of privileges for sexual favours. The more sexually explicit abuses won't be reproduced here, but are included in the report. The sadism of some of the security guards has been demonstrated by their apparent amusement at a child sewing her lips together. Despite the culture of secrecy surrounding offshore detention, the murder of Reza Barati received widespread media attention. The 24 year old Iranian died in 2014 on Manus Island, of multiple head injuries, possibly caused by a heavy object.[17] Two men were charged and found guilty of murder, but received only light sentences on the excuse that others were involved as well. These others have not been charged.[18] Reza had graduated as an architect, but due to the impact that sanctions had on Iran's economy, he was unable to find work. He left for Australia in order to further his studies.[19]

Offshore detention and 'border protection' took a decidedly military and cloak and dagger tone under 'Operation Sovereign Borders.' Some events were kept secret as 'on-water matters' and Nauru raised the price of a visa for journalists as a disincentive to visit. The 2015 Border Force Act made it illegal to disclose conditions inside detention centres, carrying a 2 year prison term. However, whistle blowers have continued to speak out. The Australian Government has continually defended its policies in court, and in February of 2016 offshore processing was found to be legal under changes to the Migration act.[20] The Australian Government has even mooted further changing the Migration Act so that refugees and asylum seekers in offshore centres would never be allowed to settle in Australia, even if they were found to be genuine refugees. It has been suggested that this appears at odds with Article 31 of the UN 1951 Convention relating to the Status of Refugees, which states that signatories 'shall not impose penalties, on account of their illegal entry or presence, on refugees.'[21] Now, not even those who arrived prior to July 2013 are safe. These people have now been given (at the time of writing) 60 days to fill in complicated forms, including all proof of identity documentation, or else risk losing payments and their ability to claim asylum. They may also lose the right to apply for a bridging visa, access to Medicare and permission to work. Deportation would then follow.[22]

President Trump's original ban on entry into the US targeted seven Muslim majority countries: Iran, Iraq, Libya, Somalia, Sudan, Syria and Yemen. This ban affected citizens of those countries and those holding green cards. The ban was removed by the courts and then a bid to reinstate the ban was blocked by a federal appeals panel under the premise that the government had failed to prove this decision advanced national security. This executive order was widely criticised as un-American and resulted in some 60,000 visas being cancelled in the days that followed. The court decision overturns this, but leaves one element untouched, the reduction of the refugee quota for 2017 from 110,000 to 50,000.[23] A revised version of the ban removes Iraq from the list of countries due to its aid in helping fight ISIS, and removes the indefinite ban of Syrian refugees.[24]

Meanwhile, in Australia, two bills put before parliament look to expand the powers of the immigration minister. The visa ban bill would prevent any adult taken to Nauru or Manus Island after 19 July 2013 from ever being able to apply for a valid Australian visa. The second bill allows the minister to issue the requirement that a whole cohort of visa holders to have their visas revalidated, for any class of visa. Such a request would stop these people from entering the country until the visa was revalidated, and also affects those already residing in Australia. The discretion for these decisions lies completely with the minister, 'in the national interest.'[25]

Do not oppress the alien

So how does the bible address issues of asylum and migration? Should Christians care about refugees? According to Scripture, we should. There are a number of texts we can examine that deal with the Old Testament idea of obligation to the stranger (*ger* in Hebrew.)[26] In Exodus 22:21 the logic is simple; the people of Israel were strangers in the land of Egypt, therefore you should not oppress (as they were in Egypt) the stranger in the land. Modern day oppression takes many forms, but mandatory detention and racial vilification all fit this bill.

Perhaps too, if we stop to realise that unless we are an Aboriginal or Torres Strait Islander, we too are strangers in the land. I will have more to say on this in chapter 5.

The gleaning law in Leviticus 19:10 groups the stranger with the needy, and allows them to gather the fallen fruit of the vineyard. Any legal decision that leaves refugees in dire need, such as preventing them from working or denying them access to health care, is therefore in contravention of this principle. In case it could be argued that these commands in spirit (if not in letter given the original context), do not apply to life beyond the physical borders of Israel, consider Leviticus 19:34, which says that 'The stranger who resides with you shall be to you as the native among you, and *you shall love him as yourself,* for you were aliens in the land of Egypt; I am the Lord your God,' emphasis mine (NASB). So when we read Jesus affirming that the second greatest commandment is to love your neighbour as yourself, and that a Samaritan could be a good neighbour, we see that any stranger is to be the subject of our love. As Jesus comes to fulfil the law, so in Christ we obey those aspects of the law fulfilled and embodied in him, but not done away with, such as the law to love.

The physical provision for the stranger is reaffirmed in Deuteronomy 14:29, together with that for the Levite, the fatherless, and the widow. All of those who could be without inheritance in the land, the Levite by command, the fatherless and the widow being left without someone to provide for their needs, were to be provided for in other ways. And not just the resident, but also the stranger or alien in their midst! Just as the parable of the Good Samaritan turned convention on its head by making a hero out of the northern neighbour of mixed race and religion, so Deuteronomy 23:7 includes the Edomite as the brother of the Israelite. Just as shockingly, the Israelite was not to detest an Egyptian, precisely because they have been aliens in Egypt! It could not be clearer that for the Christian, objecting to Muslim asylum seekers on religion alone is not permitted.

Another theme not often considered in the context of refugees is that of the Moabites. In Deuteronomy 2:9, the Israelites were told not to harass the Moabites, because the Lord has given them their land as a possession. Yet in Deuteronomy 23:2-4, the command is that no Moabite shall enter the assembly of the Lord because of the way they treated the Israelites in their wandering, not providing them with food, and seeking to have them cursed by the prophet Balaam. At times, Moab was Israel's enemy and a tool of judgment of the Lord (Judges 3:12). Yet Ruth, the Moabite daughter in law of Naomi, returned with her to Israel, to become part of the line of David, and eventually that of Jesus. Such a story demonstrates how ideas of racial purity are mythical, and how refugees can make profound contributions to society. The histories of modern Australia, Britain and the USA are littered with such stories.

Another line of argument deals with the whole concept of national boundaries. Esther Reed takes on the ethics of territorial borders, and finds that their value is somewhat ambiguous.[27] Reed considers whether or not God has set national boundaries, considering four key biblical texts. Psalm 74:17 speaks of God establishing the boundaries of the earth and the seasons, which makes the verse more of a creation text rather than a strictly political one. Likewise, Ezekiel 47:13 refers to the tribal boundaries within Israel, and is therefore concerned with the inheritance of the land more than the fate of the nations. The national boundaries that Paul mentions in his Areopagus speech in Acts 17:24-26 are set so that people might seek after God. It is therefore difficult to apply any of these texts to a theology of national boundaries, and certainly is not justification for colonialism and the boundaries that were imposed by western powers in continents like Africa. Neither can biblical passages be used to justify the dispossession in Australia of Aboriginal and Torres Strait Islander peoples under the lie of *terra nullius,* or the US understanding of North America as Canaan and the settlers as Israel. Of all the texts considered, Deuteronomy 32:8-9 appears to be the strongest assertion that territorial identity is based on divine decision, particularly with regards to Israel.

And it is on the territory of Israel that much of this discussion hangs. Reed identifies Ezekiel 47:13-14 as a key text. It speaks of the promised inheritance of the twelve tribes of Israel after the return from exile. Reed sees this prophesy as being fulfilled in Jesus' saying in Matthew 25:31-36. At the sorting of the sheep and goats, all the nations can potentially share in the inheritance. This anticipates the Great Commission of Matthew 28:16-20, where Jesus is given authority on earth and heaven (harking back yet further to the Lord's Prayer in Matthew 6:9-13). This global authority means Jesus' disciples are to make disciples of all nations. People from every nation, tribe and tongue will come to the throne of Jesus (Revelation 7:9). Tellingly, the condition under which the nations are to be judged in Matthew 25 is their treatment of strangers. In the Greek, the word is *genos*, meaning family, race, or nation. This condition Reed calls an ethic of answerability, i.e. the nations will be answerable for the way in which they treat those in need, and refugees are surely those in need. To be sure, Reed acknowledges that placing the emphasis on national boundaries and nations per se can be used to remove guilt from individuals. However, in the west we vote for our governments, and governments typically enact policies that are popular with voters. Western attitudes to refugees need to be combated both in terms of fair legislation that does not contravene international or biblical law, but also shifts in community attitudes based on the truth. Such a shift is called repentance.

The Asylum Seeker Resource Centre deals with the common myths about asylum seekers.[28] Two are worth mentioning briefly. The first is that asylum seekers are illegal immigrants. By definition, asylum seekers are not immigrants in the strict sense because they have left their country out of fear of persecution, not simply a desire to become citizens of another country. Neither are they illegal, since under the UN convention they have good cause for entering a country without a visa. Pinan Agzan and co-authors go further in their editorial in *Migration Letters* in that they see no difference between a refugee and an 'economic migrant.' They observe that 'all refugees have an obvious economic cause along with the immediate threat they are escaping from.'[29] A second myth is that which delegitimises an asylum seekers' claim based solely on their means of arrival; in the case of Australia, by boat. In recent years, about 90% of people who have arrived that way have been found to be refugees.

The fact that a small number of the people arriving by boat to Australia are not found to be genuine refugees does not justify mandatory detention, nor the laws introduced to deny anyone entry who arrives in that manner. It simply means that proper processing of asylum applications and properly regulated national borders is wise governance. Reed also affirms borders while questioning them, recognising how they maintain shared identity and common interests. She also warns of utopian visions of society with totally porous borders. We have already seen how large influxes of refugees not well handled can stir up sectarian concerns. However, in maintaining borders, the ethic of answerability applies, and Australia, the US and some European nations will be held to account.

Syria and drought

Coming back to the country under discussion at the start of this chapter, the situation in Syria is as complicated as it is dire. As Pinar Yazgan and co-authors note, Syria has been 'a country of multifaceted problems: unemployment, income inequality, suppression of minorities, suppression of opposition ....'[30] Or as Peter Gleick puts it, 'conflicts are rarely, if ever, attributable to single causes.' However, Gleick does find that water and climatic conditions have impacted Syria's economic conditions.[31] Syria is considered water scarce, with an annual average rainfall of less than 250 mm. In such a low rainfall region, rivers are critical. Unfortunately for Syria, regional water politics exists, as the country shares all of its major rivers with its neighbours. Tensions exist between Syria, Jordan and Turkey over dams and control of water. Jordan and Syria have long been at loggerheads over Syrian damming of the Yarmouk River, while the flow of the Euphrates into Syria from Turkey has declined since 1990, after the completion of the Ataturk Dam. Furthermore, as Syria's population increases, so water per person per year decreases; with an increase from 3 million people in 1950 to 22 million in 2012, renewable water availability decreased from 5500 m^3 per person per year to less than 760 m^3 per person per year. This level is categorised as scarce. Other sources of water in the region are wells from aquifers. These resources have been extensively exploited, leading to a drop in the water table and contamination of water supplies by salts and nitrates.

Drought is not unknown in Syria, with six significant droughts recorded in the period 1900 to 2005.[32] During these droughts, rainy season rainfall dropped to about a third of its normal value, but never for longer than about two seasons. However, from 2006 to 2011, Syria suffered prolonged drought, resulting in agricultural failures, disruptions to the economy, and population displacement from rural to urban areas. This period has been described as the 'worst long-term drought and most severe set of crop failures since agricultural civilizations began in the Fertile Crescent many millennia ago.'[33] A 2016 study looked in detail at 900 years of tree ring records to establish that the period 1998-2012 is the driest in the record.[34] Droughts of this order can act as multipliers of pre-existing socioeconomic pressures. Drought reduced cereal crop yields between about 50 and 70%. By late 2011, the drought had affected between 2 to 3 million people, pushing them into extreme poverty. More than 1.5 million people were forced to migrate from rural to urban areas, although some debate these numbers.[35] Indeed, across the region in the so-called 'Arab Spring,' climate change related factors have driven increasing food prices and hence political, social and economic instability.[36]

The impacts of the Syrian drought are further complicated by poor water management. Over 80% of irrigated land prior to the civil war was done by highly inefficient flood irrigation, and nearly 80% of all groundwater withdrawals in Syria are unsustainable. While the Assad regime improved access to water by building more infrastructure, Suzanne Saleeby concludes that 'the regime's failure to put in place economic measures to alleviate the effects of drought was a critical driver in propelling such massive mobilizations of dissent.'[37] Thankfully, the Australian Government continues to process the 12,000 Syrian and Iraqi refugees, under a one-off agreement announced by the former Abbott government.[38]

The climate connection

As we have seen, political instability and poor infrastructure has meant that the prolonged drought in Syria has impacted agriculture, leading to internal displacement and social unrest. The situation is complicated, but environmental stressors are implicated. In their review article, Kate

Burrows and Patrick Kinney note that the interaction between climate change, migration and conflict are complex, poorly understood, and context specific.[39] In the case of Syria, the high dependence of those displaced on agriculture appears to provide the necessary context. A 2012 study found that a decrease in wintertime Mediterranean rainfall has likely occurred during the period 1902–2010 whose magnitude cannot be explained by natural changes.[40] Ten of the twelve driest years since 1902 have occurred in the 20 years leading up to 2011. It appears that global warming has led to a change in a circulation known as the North Atlantic Oscillation, or NAO. The NAO measures the pressure difference between the low pressure system located over Iceland and the high pressure system near the Azores. The NAO determines the path that rain-bearing systems take over Europe. Warming of the atmosphere appears to have changed this circulation to steer storms over northern Europe, producing drier conditions over the Mediterranean during the cold season. This change in the NAO may be due to increases in sea surface temperatures in the Indian Ocean. There are complications with observational datasets, and much work still needs to be done. Not everyone agrees that there is a climate connection.[41] Anaïs Voski calls for caution, given that 'research and data are both fairly recent and thus should be utilized with caution.'[42] Voski also notes that finding a direct relationship between changing climate and the outbreak of civil war is ongoing. However, to date the evidence points in the direction that climate change has already changed the climate of the Mediterranean. Future climate change will only make conditions worse and, in collaboration with political factors, cause human displacement.[43]

The rising tide of climate refugees

Can we really speak of climate refugees? We've seen that the situation in Syria is complex. In fact, the issues that force people to relocate outside of their own national borders are always going to be complex. Francois Gemenne thinks that there is a valuable definition. The term 'environmental migration' shifts the emphasis from migration as a disaster to be avoided to an adaptation strategy to be facilitated. In this framework, migrants are not resourceless victims but resourceful agents. Gemenne recognises that environmental migration depoliticises such movements, but that the phrase climate refugees reaffirms the political nature of forced migration due to climate change. Those who migrate are forced to flee by environmental disruption that they have contributed little to, but to which developed nations have contributed much, a point I return to in chapter 6. It is important not to simplify the link between migration and climate, as authors Burrows and Kinney stress in their review on climate change.[44] However, as noted by climatologist Kevin Trenberth in the journal *Climatic Change*, 'The answer to the oft-asked question of whether an event is caused by climate change is that it is the wrong question. All weather events are affected by climate change because the environment in which they occur is warmer and moister than it used to be.'[45]

To this point, I have focussed on Syria for two reasons. Firstly, it is an humanitarian crisis that reveals how fragile both our systems and our compassion can be. Secondly, the Syrian crisis demonstrates how the tendrils of climate change reach into a conflict in a way we might have at first overlooked. There are other more obvious sources of climate refugees closer to home. As the climate warms, ocean waters expand and sea levels rise. Glaciers and continental ice sheets are also melting and collapsing into the ocean, adding to this rise. Although there is much uncertainty with the rate of collapse, it appears to be happening much faster than we originally thought.

Such sea level rise impacts are already being felt in South Pacific communities.[46] Rising sea level contributes to coastal erosion, causing atolls in Tuvalu to be abandoned.[47] Salt water intrusion through the porous coral that makes up the atolls has impacted taro crops, which are often now grown in tins.[48] In the low lying coastal areas of Fiji, sugar cane crops have been poor due to increasingly saline conditions. Loss of fresh water and the intrusion of salt water due to sea level rise is considered the most serious climate related risk for people in places like Kiribati.

Han Island, the main island of the Carteret group off Papua New Guinea, is home to more than 1500 people. Nicholas Hakata is an elder on Han Island. He describes life there as a holiday island paradise of fishing, checking on banana crops, or sitting around and relaxing. However, over the past few years, life has become more difficult. In 2008, Han Island was completely inundated by sea water.[49] Still bodies of water left over have been responsible for malarial outbreaks, and this, together with malnutrition, keeps children from attending school.[50] Inundation events also damage banana crops and other foods. The islanders are reliant on boats bringing in supplies, but these are unreliable. In 2007, the Carteret islanders decided to initiate a migration program to Bougainville, and land has been set aside for settlements, although progress has been slow. Han Islanders hope that they can continue to visit home, to fish on the reefs. Sadly, sea level rise, ocean warming and acidification of the waters by dissolved carbon dioxide means that this is highly unlikely.

Of course, people don't want to move from their island homes. They don't choose to become climate change refugees as a lifestyle option. One Tuvaluan expresses it this way: 'We don't want to leave this place. We don't want to leave, it's our land, our God given land, it is our culture, we can't leave. People won't leave until the very last minute.' The last thing people want to become is a refugee: 'Moving away from Tuvalu is not good for our culture and values. We want to live in our own land, our home and where our forefathers have lived. Tuvaluan people don't like to be called refugees.'[51] Note the strong link between a theology of place, land, and culture.

Sometimes this largely Christian worldview places people in denial. Two Tuvaluan school girls insisted that they did not believe in climate change; 'No. We're Christians. God will protect the island.' One man proclaimed; 'Only the Creator can flood the world … I believe in God—I don't believe in scientists.'[52] For others, it can cause them to question God's faithfulness, 'We plant and depend on God to provide fruits. We go out fishing with faith that God will provide enough daily. The failure of these seems to indicate to the people that God's providence has failed them.' Some Tuvaluans fail to understand that sea level rise is not God's wrath upon them, but the consequence of human behaviour and injustice that is responsible for the changes they observe. Instead, like ancient Israel, they see a direct link between their relationship with God and blessing and cursing.[53] Whatever the precise theology, whenever the religious faith over Pacific (or Oceania) peoples is ignored, climate change projects there fail.[54]

So, how many people will be affected by climate change and made into climate refugees by sea level rise? The estimates vary wildly, but ignoring the high end estimate that is sometimes considered alarmist (which doesn't make it out of the realms of possibility), 1 metre sea level rise could create 50 million environmental refugees. From Norman Myers' extrapolations, as many as 200 million could be impacted. Climate change needs to be halted in its tracks. However, even if the warming of the planet stopped tomorrow, sea level rise would continue as glaciers and ice sheets will continue to melt. How many more Alan Kurdis do we need to see in the media before we realise climate change needs to be taken seriously, and its victims treated well?

Loving the alien[55]
Responding to crises

Given that we have spent so much time on the Syrian crisis, it would be remiss not to focus on what is happening there, and how Christians can support people on the ground while displaced internally or in Europe. As World Vision Australia pointed out in 2016, more than 16 million Syrians need humanitarian assistance. This figure includes 4.8 million people who have had to flee Syria. Half of all those affected are children. In 2016, World Vision was able to aid 2.3 million people, including those inside Syria and neighbouring countries. This aid included helping people access food, clean water, sanitation and hygiene services, providing shelter and emergency supplies such as blankets and warm winter clothing, and trying to bring some normalcy into children's lives by providing safe spaces to learn, play and receive other forms of support. World Vision is asking that the 'international community must step up and use all diplomatic influence at its disposal to ensure these attacks stop and children and families can access lifesaving assistance.' This does not include bombs!

Ultimately, people do not want to flee their own countries to become refugees, and what will be required is a monumental political solution. Praying and writing to politicians to do more diplomatically is required.

However, while the conflict continues, giving generously to support people in need is a matter of justice.

To help, see

https://www.worldvision.com.au/global-issues/world-emergencies/ syrian-refugee-crisis
http://www.wvi.org/syria-crisis/article/donate-now

Love makes a way

Australia has a well-documented and internationally condemned policy of offshore detention and processing of refugees. Love Makes A Way (LMAW) is, in their own words, 'a movement of Christians seeking an end to Australia's inhumane asylum seeker policies through prayer and nonviolent love in action.' LMAW began in March of 2014, following the murder of Reza Berati in February of that year. At the time, there were 1138 children in immigration detention centres. The first action was conceived of in a pub in Paddington (aren't all good ideas conceived of in a pub?) The result has been numerous pray-ins, groups of Christians making themselves at home in politicians' offices to pray and to seek to speak to them about these inhumane policies.

Sam McLean, the former National Director of GetUp! wrote that

'The public narrative on refuge in Australia has been dominated for the last five years by frames of fear and the idea that we must 'be cruel to be kind.' Love Makes A Way is the only effort cutting through that at the moment. They are brave, but more than that, they're smart, careful, and deliberate. They have consistently generated public attention, but the real art has been to do so in a way that is entirely on their message and their terms.'

LMAW is a powerful testimony to the power of the non-violent gospel of Jesus, and his heart for justice. You can learn more about the campaign and donate at http://lovemakesaway.org.au/.

Sanctuary

In the US, an increasingly strong stance has been taken towards refugees, foreign visitors and immigrants. As the Sanctuary Movement website states

'As faith allies, we are called to be in solidarity through rapid response mobilization to stop these raids, stop these deportations and support impacted communities. In the face of President Trump's extremist anti-immigrant agenda we must respond with a prophetic and bold voice.' The movement in the US includes congregations from a variety of traditions, including Catholic, Quaker, Unitarian, Mormon, Jewish, Episcopalian and Methodist. The pledge is non-specific in its faith claims, but upholds the principles of justice and loving your neighbour

'As people of faith and people of conscience, we pledge to resist the newly elected administration's policy proposals to target and deport millions of undocumented immigrants and discriminate against marginalized communities. We will open up our congregations and communities as sanctuary spaces for those targeted by hate, and work alongside our friends, families, and neighbors to ensure the dignity and human rights of all people.'

However, as Noel Anderson, an ordained pastor in the United Church of Christ points out, 'There is, across Abrahamic faith traditions at least, this dictate to welcome the stranger, for you were once a stranger in the land of Egypt. What are faith communities if not sanctuaries?'[56] Our faith has deep reserves to draw upon on this issue, and the need for justice is great.

For more information see http://www.sanctuarynotdeportation.org/.

Endnotes

1 Lucy Rodgers, David Gritten, James Offer and Patrick Asare, "Syria: The story of the conflict," *BBC News*, 11 March, 2016, accessed 25 February, 2017, http://www.bbc.com/news/world-middle-east-26116868.

2 Helena Smith, "Shocking images of drowned Syrian boy show tragic plight of refugees," *The Guardian*, 3 September, 2015, accessed 25 February, 2017, https://www.theguardian.com/world/2015/sep/02/shocking-image-of-drowned-syrian-boy-shows-tragic-plight-of-refugees.

3 Adrian Raschella, "Former SAS commander breaks silence on Tampa," *ABC News*, 8 July, 2011, accessed 26 February, 2017, http://www.abc.net.au/news/2011-07-07/former-sas-commander-breaks-silence-on-tampa/2785164.

4 Gwynne Dyer, "Europe's refugee crisis: The good, the bad, and the ugly," *The Sydney Morning Herald*, 3 September, 2015, accessed 26 February, 2017, http://www.smh.com.au/comment/eu-response-to-migrant-crisis-ranges-from-generosity-to-panic-20150903-gje39e.html.

5   Kate Lyons, "UK unlikely to reach target of resettling 20,000 Syrian refugees," *The Guardian*, 3 August, 2016, accessed 26 February, 2017, https://www.theguardian.com/politics/2016/aug/03/uk-unlikely-to-reach-target-of-resettling-20000-syrian-refugees-by-2020.

6   Gwynne Dyer, *Europe's refugee crisis*.

7   Nick Robins-Early, "Europe's Anti-Refugee Parties Are Dangerous Even When They Don't Win," *Worldpost*, 31 May, 2016, accessed 26 February, 2017, http://www.huffingtonpost.com/entry/europe-far-right-austria_us_5745c61fe4b03ede4413710a.

8   Gregor Aisch, Adam Pearce, and Bryant Rousseau, "How Far Is Europe Swinging to the Right?" *The New York Times*, 5 December, 2016, accessed 26 February, 2017, https://www.nytimes.com/interactive/2016/05/22/world/europe/europe-right-wing-austria-hungary.html.

9   Robins-Early, *Europe's Anti-Refugee Parties*.

10   Aisch, Pearce, and Rousseau, *How Far Is Europe Swinging to the Right?*

11   Amanda Marcotte, "Donald Trump and the European far right," *Salon*, 28 January, 2017, accessed 26 February, 2017, http://www.salon.com/2017/01/28/europe-2/.

12   Christine Hauser, "Donald Trump Jr. compares Syrian refugees to Skittles that 'would kill you'," *The New York Times*, September 20, 2016, accessed December 21, 2016, http://www.nytimes.com/2016/09/21/us/politics/donald-trump-jr-faces-backlash-after-comparing-syrian-refugees-to-skittles-that-can-kill.html.

13   Georgina Mitchell, "Q&A: Naomi Klein says Australia no better than 'insane and racist' Donald Trump," *The Sydney Morning Herald*, 8 November, 2016, accessed 19 February, 2017.

14   Helen Davidson, "Offshore detention: Australia's recent immigration history a 'human rights catastrophe'," *The Guardian*, 13 November, 2016, accessed 26 February, 2017, https://www.theguardian.com/australia-news/2016/nov/13/offshore-detention-nauru-immigration-history-human-rights.

15   Cited in Davidson, *Offshore detention*.

16   Paul Farrell, Nick Evershed, and Helen Davidson, "The Nauru files: cache of 2,000 leaked reports reveal scale of abuse of children in Australian offshore detention," *The Guardian*, 10 August, 2016, accessed 26 February, 2017, https://www.theguardian.com/australia-news/2016/aug/10/the-nauru-files-2000-leaked-reports-reveal-scale-of-abuse-of-children-in-australian-offshore-detention.

17   Paul Farrell, "Asylum seeker Reza Barati died from 'multiple head injuries', PNG police say," *The Guardian*, 26 February, 2014, accessed 26 February, 2017, https://www.theguardian.com/world/2014/feb/26/asylum-seeker-reza-barati-died-from-multiple-head-injuries-png-police-say.

18   Ben Doherty and Helen Davidson, "Reza Barati: men convicted of asylum seeker's murder to be free in less than four years," *The Guardian*, 19 April, 2016, accessed 26 February, 2017, https://www.theguardian.com/australia-news/2016/apr/19/reza-barati-men-convicted-of-asylum-seekers-to-be-free-in-less-than-four-years.

19   Paul McGeough, "Someone's son, someone's brother: Reza Barati, an architect who

had hopes for a better life," *The Sydney Morning Herald*, 1 March, 2014, accessed 26 February, 2017, http://www.smh.com.au/national/someones-son-someones-brother-reza-barati-an-architect-who-had-hopes-for-a-better-life-20140228-33r4n.html.

20 Davidson, *Offshore detention*.

21 Stephanie Anderson, "How is the Government changing Australia's immigration policy?" *ABC News*, 7 November, 2016, accessed 26 February, 2017, http://www.abc. net.au/news/2016-11-07/how-is-the-government-changing-australias-immigration-policy/7996964.

22 Michael Kozioi, "'Draconian and dangerous': Despair over fresh crackdown on asylum seekers," *The Sydney Morning Herald*, 26 February, 2017, accessed 26 February, 2017, http://www.smh.com.au/federal-politics/political-news/draconian-and-dangerous-despair-over-fresh-crackdown-on-asylum-seekers-20170223-guk3of.html.

23 Adam Lipta, "Court Refuses to Reinstate Travel Ban, Dealing Trump Another Legal Loss," *The New York Times*, 9 February, 2017, accessed 2 March, 2017, https://www. nytimes.com/2017/02/09/us/politics/appeals-court-trump-travel-ban.html.

24 Matthew Lee, and Vivian Salama, "Donald Trump's 'Muslim ban' to be re-introduced with Iraq removed from list of countries," *The Independent*, 1 March, 2017, accessed 2 March, 2017, http://www.independent.co.uk/news/world/americas/us-politics/donald-trump-muslim-ban-immigration-reform-change-iraq-countries-a7604926.html.

25 Elizabeth Colliver, Lauren Bull and Shawn Rajanayagam, "Think Trump's travel ban was bad? Peter Dutton may soon have the power to play God," *The Guardian*, 1 March, 2017, accessed 2 March, 2017, https://www.theguardian.com/commentisfree/2017/mar/01/think-trumps-travel-ban-was-bad-peter-dutton-may-soon-have-the-power-to-play-god.

26 Mark G. Brett, "Forced migration, asylum seekers, and human rights," *Colloquium* 45:2 (2013): 121-136.

27 Esther D. Reed, "Refugee Rights and State Sovereignty: Theological Perspectives on the Ethics of Territorial Borders," *Journal of the Society of Christian Ethics* 30:2 (2010): 59-78.

28 Asylum Seeker Resource Centre, *Asylum seekers and refugees: myths, facts + solutions* (West Melbourne: Asylum Seeker Resource Centre). Accessed 2 March, 2017, https:// www.asrc.org.au/pdf/myths-facts-solutions-info_.pdf.

29 Pinar Yazgan, Deniz Eroglu Utku, and Ibrahim Sirkeci, "Editorial: Syrian Crisis and Migration," *Migration Letters* 12 (2015): 181-192.

30 Yazga, Utku, and Sirkeci, *Editorial*.

31 Peter H. Gleick, 'Water, Drought, Climate Change, and Conflict in Syria,' *Weather, Climate, and Society* 6 (2014): 331-340.

32 Colin P. Kelley, Shahrzad Mohtadi, Mark A. Cane, Richard Seager, and Yochanan Kushnir, "Climate change in the Fertile Cresent and implications of the recent Syrian drought," *Proceedings of the National Academy of Science* 112:11 (2015): 3241-3246.

33 Francesco Femia, and Caitlin Werrell, "Syria: Climate Change, Drought and Social Unrest," *The Center for Climate and Security*, 29 February, 2012, accessed 9 march, 2017, https://climateandsecurity.org/2012/02/29/syria-climate-change-drought-and-social-unrest/.

34 Benjamin L. Cook, Kevin J. Anchukatis, Ramzi Touchan, David M. Meko, and Edward R. Cook, "Spatiotemporal drought variability in the Mediterranean over the last 900 years," *Journal of Geophysical Research: Atmospheres* 121 (2016): 2060-2074.

35 Jan Selby, and Mike Hulme, "Is climate change really to blame for Syria's civil war?" *The Guardian*, 30 November, 2015, accessed 23 July, 2017, https://www.theguardian.com/commentisfree/2015/nov/29/climate-change-syria-civil-war-prince-charles.

36 Ines Perez, "Climate Change and Rising Food Prices Heightened Arab Spring," *Scientific American*, 4 March, 2013, accessed 3 June, 2017, https://www.scientificamerican.com/article/climate-change-and-rising-food-prices-heightened-arab-spring/.

37 Suzanne Saleeby, "Sowing the Seeds of Dissent: Economic Grievances and the Syrian Social Contract's Unravelling," *Yadaliyya* February 16, 2012. Accessed 25 February, 2017, http://www.jadaliyya.com/pages/index/4383/sowing-the-seeds-of-dissent_economic-grievances-an.

38 Anderson, *How is the Government changing Australia's immigration policy?*

39 Michael Brzoska and Christiane Fröhlich, "Climate change, migration and violent conflict: vulnerabilities, pathways and adaptation strategies," *Migration and Development* 5:2 (2016): 190-210.

40 Martin Hoerling, Jon Eischeid, Judith Perlwitz, Xiaowei Quan, Tao Zhang, and Philip Pegion, "On the Increased Frequency of Mediterranean Drought," *Journal of Climate* 25 (2012): 2146-2161.

41 Selby and Hulme, *Is climate change really to blame*.

42 Anaïs Voski, "The Role of Climate Change in Armed Conflicts across the Developing World and in the Ongoing Syrian War," *Carleton Review of International Affairs* 3 (2016): 120-141.

43 Gleick, *Water, Drought, Climate Change*.

44 Kate Burrows, and Patrick L. Kinney, "Exploring the Climate Change, Migration and Conflict Nexus," *International Journal of Environmental Research and Public Health* 13 (2016), doi:10.3390/ijerph13040443.

45 Kevin E. Trenberth, "Framing the way to relate climate extremes to climate change," *Climatic Change* 115:2 (2012): 283-290.

46 I examined this more in Mick Pope, "Climate Change in Oceania: Ecomission and ecojustice," *Lausanne Global Analysis*, 3:2 (2014), accessed 9 March, 2017, https://www.lausanne.org/content/lga/2014-03/climate-change-in-oceania-ecomission-and-ecojustice.

47 C.A. Moore, "Awash in a rising sea—How global warming is overwhelming the islands of the tropical Pacific," *International Wildfire* Jan-Feb 2002.

48 Tuvalu's National Adaptation Programme of Action, Ministry of Natural Resources, Environment, Agriculture and Lands. Department of Environment. May 2007. unfccc.int/resource/docs/napa/tuv01.pdf. Last accessed 11 November, 2013.

49 Julie Edwards, "The Carteret Islands: First man-made climate change evacuees still await resettlement," Pacific Conference of Churches, November 2010, accessed 11 November, 2013, http://www.pcc.org.fj/docs/Julias%20Cartaret.pdf.

50   United Nations University, "Local solutions on a sinking paradise, Carteret Islands, Papua New Guinea." http://vimeo.com/4177527, last accessed 11 November, 2013.

51   Friends of the Earth International, *Climate Change: Voices from Communities Affected by Climate Change* (Amsterdam: Friends of the Earth, 2007).

52   Mark Lynas, *High Tide: News from a Warming Planet* (London: Flamingo, 2004).

53   Ruth Moon, "Teaching Natural Theology as Climate Changes Drown A Way of Life." Posted 14/2/2012, accessed 11 November, 2013, http://www.christianitytoday.com/ct/2012/february/natural-theology-climate-change.html.

54   Patrick D. Nunn, "Sidelining God: why secular climate projects in the Pacific Islands are failing," *The Conversation*, 17 May, 2017, accessed 3 June, 2017, https://theconversation.com/sidelining-god-why-secular-climate-projects-in-the-pacific-islands-are-failing-77623.

55   Other than a reference to the many passages in the Old Testament, the older reader or music aficionado may recognise the reference to a David Bowie song.

56   Dwyer Gunn, "The sanctuary movement: how religious groups are sheltering the undocumented," *The Guardian*, 8 February, 2017, accessed 11 April, 2017, https://www.theguardian.com/us-news/2017/feb/08/sanctuary-movement-undocumented-immigrants-america-trump-obama.

CHAPTER 5 — MIND THE GAP

You and your racist friend

I tend to waste a fair amount of time on social media. Facebook has been both a blessing and a curse. It can be a huge echo chamber if we let it, so having a diverse set of friends can be a good thing. But like most, I've had to defriend a few people from time to time. The reasons vary, but in a couple of cases it's been when racism rears its ugly head. I'm not claiming to be the most enlightened person around, scratch a little deeper and many of us have fear and insecurities. But I am grateful for the things I have learned and the people I have met. And if Reconciliation is to occur in this country, real and practical as well as what is often dismissed as 'symbolic', then we all need to keep walking on a journey together.

One Facebook 'friend' suggested that since Europeans had arrived, the Aboriginal and Torres Strait Islander peoples no longer had a say in the way our country operates. Their opinion no longer carried weight due to sheer numbers of non-Indigenous Australians. Even my son, who was 12 years old at the time, could tell that this was racist. I quoted him in my 'I'm defriending you' message with the *They Might Be Giants* song, *You and your racist friend* running through my head. The other occasion was the altogether typical vitriol directed against AFL player Adam Goodes, not long after he was racially vilified on field. It doesn't take much to reveal the racist underbelly of Australian society, as was in evidence in the treatment he received. I wouldn't have minded if it was a fair discussion about the role of politics in sport, or if there was a real case to be made about Goodes' on-field behaviour. Instead, all I read was racism, emotive labelling, and not even the semblance of honest debate. Adam Goodes had hit a nerve and this person was screaming in rage. Let's repeat what happened; an Aboriginal sportsman was called out for celebrating a goal with an Aboriginal war dance, during Indigenous round. The cheek of him! And then to top it all off, he didn't let a young girl get away with calling him an ape. How dare he? Poor little girl. I hope you get sarcasm. Let's face it, all of the arguments mounted about how Adam used to milk penalties, was grandstanding, picking on the child, and illegitimately bringing politics into sport have all been demolished.[1] But did those arguments even matter? He was vilified because he is Aboriginal and won't keep quiet about it.

And this leads me to a third incident, although to date the person remains a 'friend' on Facebook. They shared a meme, hardly the most sophisticated way of spreading ideas. It said in essence that Sorry Day was about people not guilty of anything apologising to people no longer affected by the events being apologised for. I'm guessing that this person thinks that the gap in health, employment, and life expectancy are all down to genetic defects or lifestyle choices alone. Perhaps they think that Aboriginal and Torres Strait Islander peoples are just way more criminally inclined to be so over represented in our prison population. Or maybe he needs to be introduced to the Wurundjeri elder whose grandmother was born on a mission at Healesville. Just two generations ago, people were removed from their homelands and corralled out of the way.[2] Or perhaps I could introduce him to my Aboriginal friend, who when I first met her over 10 years ago, didn't know of her heritage. Her grandparents chose to hide it to make life easier for their children. Tell me again that Sorry Day means nothing? Every time I used the internet to research this chapter, if I read the comments on newspaper articles, I regretted it. I uncovered ignorance of history, ignorance of the facts, and blindness to the harms done. It is time to examine history afresh.

Aboriginal culture is the oldest surviving material culture in the world, dating back over 60,000 years. There is evidence of petroglyphs, stone carvings that potentially go back this far, and are among the earliest representation of human faces.[3] They also contain images of animals found in the area before the end of the last ice age. Aboriginal peoples engaged in sophisticated land management using fire.[4] In Victoria, they engaged in eel aquaculture using a series of traps, and lived in permanent stone dwellings.[5] Aboriginal peoples have occupied every part of Australia and dealt with major climatic shifts over the past 60,000 years. As a people they have been innovative and resilient.

The impacts of colonisation

This chapter can't possibly say everything there is to be said about over 200 years of occupation and the many issues that Aboriginal and Torres Strait Islander peoples face today, nor can it look at the complexity and diversity of their situations. That, I think, is done well in Stan Grant's Quarterly Essay.[6] The focus of this chapter is on remote communities in particular, who are vulnerable to the impacts of climate change, and how this will affect the goals of closing the gap. In this, the aim is not to paint Aboriginal and Torres Strait Islander peoples as a homogeneous group (hence the use of the plural 'peoples' throughout this chapter), fetishize them or entertain a white Messiah complex. Far from it. I want to stress the resilience of Aboriginal peoples who have adapted successfully to life on what has been seen from a western point of view as a hard continent, and flourished for 60,000 years; who have survived over 200 years of colonisation, and who have some of the tools to deal with the coming change of climate. Likewise in the case of 5000 years of occupation and flourishing by Torres Strait Islander peoples. I simply want to point out that as a matter of justice, we need to recognise the injustices that have been visited upon these peoples as a direct consequence of colonialism, how climate change will exacerbate the impacts of these injustices, and why we, as their guests, need to address these issues urgently.

There is a gap between Aboriginal and Torres Strait Islander peoples and the non-Indigenous peoples of Australia. This gap represents the difference in key indicators such as health, education and employment. The Closing the Gap campaign goes back to a key report by the then Aboriginal and Torres Strait Islander Social Justice Commissioner Tom Calma, *Social Justice Report 2005.*[7] The report called for Australian governments to commit to achieving equality for Aboriginal and Torres Strait Islander peoples in the areas of health and life expectancy by 2030. The Close the Gap Coalition is a group of Aboriginal and Torres Strait Islander and non-Indigenous health and community organisations who are calling on governments to achieve these outcomes.[8] The targets are:

*   Close the gap in life expectancy within a generation. This gap is currently about 10-17 years.

- Halve the gap in mortality rates for children under five within a decade.
- Ensure all four years-olds in remote communities have access to early childhood education within five years.
- Halve the gap for students in reading, writing and numeracy within a decade.
- Halve the gap for students in year 12 attainment or equivalent attainment rates by 2020.
- Halve the gap in employment outcomes within a decade.

A 2016 newspaper article highlights a number of areas where Aboriginal and Torres Strait Islander peoples disadvantage still exists.[9] Firstly, the life expectancy goal is lagging behind. However, the article suggests that there has been a decline in mortality from chronic and circulatory diseases, and that these changes will take some years to be made clear in the statistics. Secondly, between 2010 and 2014, 505 Aboriginal and Torres Strait Islander babies died. The gap is down 83% since 1998, but is still 6.4 deaths per 1000 compared to 3.6 for Australians in general. Thirdly, 60% of students in years 7 and 8 complete year 12, compared to 86.5% for non-Indigenous Australians. This is up from 32% in the late 90s. This is a success worth celebrating, but there is much more work to be done. Fourthly, the employment rate has gone backwards, from 53.8% in 2008 to 47.5%, compared to the overall rate of 72.1%.

Incarceration rates are also alarmingly high. Aboriginal and Torres Strait Islander peoples make up 3% of the Australian population but more than 25% of the prison population. An Aboriginal man is 15 more times as likely as a non-Aboriginal man to be jailed. Among juveniles between 10 to 17 year olds, 54% of detainees are Aboriginal or Torres Strait Islander. On an average night, 34 in every 10,000 Aboriginal and Torres Strait Islander young people are in prison, compared to 1.3 per 10,000 of non-Indigenous youth.[10] Finally, Aboriginal and Torres Strait Islander youth have the highest suicide rates in the world.[11] This gap is intolerable, and should concern all Christians.

Beds are burning

I'm a bit of a Midnight Oil fan. It seems to me that their song *Beds Are Burning* covers some of the basic ideas involved in responding to the enduring legacy of colonisation and the closing of the gap.[12] Fair's fair means paying rent, financial reparations for land that was never ceded, never given up, but declared by Europeans under the lie of *Terra Nullius* to be empty, and then stolen. Next time you hear someone talk about not being able to support 'lifestyle choices' you might want to point this out. However, this rent is not just about payments of money, but opportunities to generate income, sustainable communities where people flourish in health, education, employment, and life expectancy. In other words, the gap is closed. The other line in *Beds Are Burning* of note is 'it belongs to them - let's give it back.' The undoing of the impacts of *Terra Nullius* means recognition of traditional custodianship, and return of lands to the traditional custodians. Genuine justice means land rights.

So what kind of theological approach can we construct for our burning bed? What is required is a decolonialised theology, which allows largely Aboriginal and Torres Strait Islander peoples to speak to non-Indigenous peoples of Australia. Such a theology firstly acknowledges that God was already making Godself known through creation before the arrival of Europeans. This understanding is what we read in Genesis 14:18-23, where Abram acknowledges God through an Indigenous name recognised by the priest Melchizedek, 'God Most High.'[13] This means that God was known by the people as the Creator Spirit, before God was known as Jesus. Secondly, a decolonialised theology needs to shift from the gospel of Jesus as bound up in white culture, not 'God as a white man's God or a God that the missionaries brought to us, but as our God who has lived with us in history.'[14] Jesus is the Creator Spirit who took human form and, as summed up by the Rainbow Spirit Elders, can be understood as having 'built a humpy among us.'[15] What follows here is clearly not this fully decolonialised theology, since I'm a white fella. This chapter is primarily an attempt at a conversation between non-Indigenous peoples. It acknowledges the harms done by colonisation and *Terra Nullius*, and how we might be involved in recognising and going part way towards undoing it. In other words, how do I be a good neighbour to those whose land was taken from them, and at whose expense I have lived a privileged life?

The first principle I think is helpful is that of Jubilee. In 1999, the Catholic Bishops of Australia released a statement for Social Justice Sunday about 2000 as a Jubilee year, and included a strong message about past and present injustices, Reconciliation, and land rights.[16] Jubilee takes its name from the Hebrew *yobel*, named after the trumpet that was sounded to mark the beginning of the year (Leviticus 25:9-10). Jubilee was the time when the land was to lie fallow, and wild animals could eat from it. All debts would be forgiven, and it is perhaps in this context that we can understand the phrase about debts in the Lord's Prayer in Matthew 6, that Jesus was proclaiming Jubilee. Indeed, this is explicit in Luke 4:18-20 where Jesus claims to fulfil the promise of Jubilee in Isaiah, 'the favourable year of the Lord.' Jubilee was also the year when ancestral land was returned. As a largely agrarian society, land in Israel was essential to people's way of life. It was the Israelite's inheritance from God to meet their needs. This is why Naboth did not want to sell his vineyard to King Ahab, who resorted to violence to obtain it (1 Kings 21). Just as Elijah could say to Ahab, 'have you killed, and also taken possession,' so too this message applies to the first European settlers in Australia. [17] It applies also to all who continue to maintain the dispossession and violence they began. This point has been made clear by Aboriginal Pastor Ray Minniecon, who applies Deuteronomy 32:8 to the possession of the Land by Aboriginal peoples, 'When the Most High gave the nations their inheritance, When He separated the sons of man, He set the boundaries of the peoples, according to the number of the sons of Israel.' Minniecon argues that the Aboriginal Tent Embassy in Canberra is a continual reminder of this verse, and that 'our Lands were never ceded by our ancestors.'[18]

In the New Testament, we can see that Jesus brings Jubilee, and therefore as his people we are to exercise it. Applying Jubilee principles to the concept of *Terra Nullius* exposes it as a lie, 'a horrendous distortion of truth, the claim that the land was unoccupied, that it was no-one's country.'[19] Instead, Jubilee asserts that the land (and oceans) belongs to Aboriginal and Torres Strait Islander peoples, and vice versa. In the context of *Rainbow Spirit Theology*, and the recognition of the presence of God in the land and oceans before European arrival, we can understand Acts 17:26-27 as relevant here, 'From one ancestor he made all nations to inhabit the whole earth, and he allotted the times of their existence and the boundaries of the places where they would live, so that they would search for God and perhaps grope for him and find him—though indeed he is not far from each one of us (NRSV).'

Recognising Jubilee in the Australian context means the returning of what rightfully belongs to Aboriginal and Torres Strait Islander peoples. There is no biblical warrant for the dispossession and violence that has been done. In the US, the language of conquest and Promised Land was historically applied illegitimately, of course.[20] Instead, Jubilee as an act of *mishpat* is our biblical guide.

Following on from this, Australian Old Testament scholar Mark Brett challenges applying an Israelite model for thinking about relationships between church and state or non-Indigenous to Aboriginal and Torres Strait churches.[21] While few Christians would openly suggest that the church functions as the new Israel dictating to society, many people work actively with this model in politics, and often the white church can do so with Aboriginal and Torres Strait Islander Christians. Instead, Brett suggests we follow the example of King Cyrus, allowing religious freedom. This understanding frees the church from feeling like it needs to pull the levers of state. It also rebukes the church over its historical suppression of Aboriginal and Torres Strait Islander beliefs, and allows space for the development of Aboriginal and Torres Strait Islander theologies. This latter point is important. All theology is contextualised, including our own, a point we often fail to notice. The development of Aboriginal and Torres Strait Islander theologies is essential for dealing with past injustices and true Reconciliation.

This leads finally to Peter Lewis' idea of acting in solidarity.[22] A theology of solidarity recognises that the incarnation or enfleshing of God expresses the 'radical solidarity of God.' In communion, we are called into solidarity with the crucified under grace. This also calls us, according to Lewis, in solidarity with the crucified of the world.

This provides the church with ways of knowing that runs counter to that of *Terra Nullius* which, while overturned in theory through Mabo, continues on in the battles such as the Adani coalmine. Solidarity means moving beyond paternalism to partnership. It also means examining our own privilege, and because of that, focuses on the centrality of the poor and dispossessed. Such solidarity has been in evidence between former US veterans, and the Standing Rock Sioux tribe who at the centre of the North Dakota oil pipeline protests in the US. But more of that later.

Having now examined some of the issues facing Aboriginal and Torres Strait Islander peoples as intolerable injustices and a continuation of colonisation, we acknowledge the church at large needs to walk alongside our brothers and sisters to close the gap. It is a matter of restorative justice: it is their right. While identifying the various issues and combating them, we also need to realise that climate change is, and will continue to be, a major factor.

Sea level rise in the Torres Strait

Water becomes less dense as it warms, and as the oceans warm in response to rising greenhouse gas concentrations, so sea level rises. This is known as thermal expansion, and has been the major driver of sea level rise to date. Other sources that will become more significant as time goes on are the melting of glaciers and the Greenland and Antarctic ice sheets. There is a lot of uncertainty in how long it will take ice sheets to collapse, but every new observation tends to indicate things are happening faster than we previously thought. The rate of sea level rise varies from place to place due to ocean currents and land rising as the ice sheets on top of it melts. Ground based measurements show a globally averaged rise from 1870 to 2000 of about 200 mm, whereas satellite measurements show a rise from 1993, when observations began, to September 2016 of 811 mm.[23] Sea level rise is getting faster.

How much sea level will rise depends upon the emission scenario, i.e. how much CO_2 we pump into the atmosphere. The fifth assessment report of the Intergovernmental Panel on Climate Change (IPCC) suggested that the mean value for a scenario that keeps us below 2° C of warming would produce about 40 cm of sea level rise by the end of century, with up to 55 cm possible. Of course, we are struggling to meet this commitment, while Pacific Island nations wanted 1.5° C to ensure their futures. The higher end scenarios could bring about 80 cm of sea level rise according to the IPCC.[24] The problem is, the science has moved on.

Ice sheet melt and collapse is happening faster than predicted. It is, of course, irreversible (at least on timescales you and I can easily get our heads around). Today we are seeing sea level rise in the order of a few millimetres per year. As ice starts to melt apace, rises of centimetres per year are expected. The IPCC estimates for the end of century may have to be doubled according to more recent research.[25] And always remember that end of century means just that. Not only would a 2° C world be 'decidedly warmer than the Earth has been in millions of years,' in the geologic past it has been associated with sea levels some 20 metres above present levels.[26] This means that in a few centuries, sea level would reach these levels. Not much of a long term legacy for our generation to leave behind.

It is with all that in mind that we approach the Torres Strait. The Torres Strait consists of over one hundred islands, eighteen of which are inhabited, and two mainland communities are situated on the northern peninsula. The islands are scattered over 48,000 km², from Cape York, northward to the borders of Papua New Guinea and Indonesia.[27] The Torres Strait is home to some 8,700 people, who possess distinct cultures compared to the 300 Aboriginal nations. [28] Eight thousand years ago, sea level was some 100 m lower, and the Torres Strait was only 20 m deep. Travel across the Strait was much easier, and the islands came to be populated by Melanesian people from the north.[29] Mer Island in the Torres Strait was the home of Eddie Mabo, probably the most well-known rights campaigners among non-Indigenous Australians, who was central to the overturning of the legal fiction of *Terra Nullius*.

Because the islands are very close to sea level, they are vulnerable to sea level rise. A 2010 CSIRO report found that between 1993 and 2010, sea level rose by 6 millimetres per year.[30] This is compared to the global average of 3.22 millimetres per year. While sea level rise itself is a threat, it is sea level rise combined with so-called king tides.

King tides are already a problem. Joseph Elu, chairman of the Torres Strait Regional Authority notes that 'What happened there on the one instance that water spout came down is now happening twice or three times a year in the full moon high tide months of December, January and February.'[31] Under climate change, it is likely that tropical cyclones will become more intense, adding to the problems of sea level rise with their associated storm tides.

Drought complicates issues of sea level rise. During the normally rainy season of 2015, Joseph Elu observed that 'The weather patterns have changed. We usually get storms this time of the year but we haven't had one yet.' The lack of rainfall means that the soils are not washed clean of salt left over from previous inundations, and sea level rise means inundation occurs more often. Such inundation affects houses and infrastructure, including roads and sewage systems, community facilities, traditional gardens and coastal ecosystems.[32] Cultural sites, including cemeteries, are also threatened, as occurred in the local graveyard on Saibai in 2012.[33]

Apart from impacts to the islands themselves, ocean warming is also an issue. The 2010 CSIRO report noted that the average annual sea surface temperatures in the region have risen by about 0.16-0.18° C per decade from 1950 to 2010. Rising temperatures have been bleaching coral reefs globally.[34] Such events impact tourism and fisheries as sources of protein.

It is acknowledged by locals that eventually they may face the likelihood of migration. However, Joseph Elu notes that 'the last option I suppose is relocation but most of the island people don't want to do that.'[35] Saibai elder Mebai Warusam is typical of this attitude, 'I will never move from this island. I will jump on my boat, tie that rope on a wongai tree. I will live here; I will die here.'[36] Migration is not a desirable option, as discussed in the last chapter. As Elaine Kelley laments, 'the material damages expose a deeper and more profound cultural impact for Islander communities. The line between adapting and enduring loss is blurred in this situation, revealing a deeply troubling limit to adaptation.' This is because, as Kelley further observes, complete loss of islands like Saibai and the resulting forced migrations 'poses a significant threat to the transmission of their people's culture, tied as it is to place.'[37] The fear of forced migration has now been termed 'Solastalgia,' being homesick while still being at home.[38]

In the shorter term, there are plans in place for building community adaptive capacity and resilience, and the Torres Strait Regional Authority has been instrumental in contributing to these plans. The most recent report notes that the communities possess a number of strengths that will help them deal with the challenges of climate change, including 'a very healthy and intact natural environment, a strong cultural connection to, and traditional knowledge of, that environment, relatively good community cohesion and leadership.'[39] This can be combined with western science-based programs, such as early warning systems, to build resilience for weather related events.

The climate change strategy includes physical adaptations to sea level rise such as coastal planning, implementing setbacks for new development, managing sand dunes and their vegetation, raising housing, raising and filling inundation prone areas, building seawalls and levees and groynes (a rigid structure designed to limit the movement of sediment), and beach nourishment, i.e. replacing eroded sand. As well as using western scientific methods to monitor changes in ecosystem, atmosphere and ocean in the region, the strategy also calls for respect for Ailan Kastom (island custom), the acknowledgment of native title rights, and the promotion of cultural and traditional knowledge. The strategy is worth quoting at length:

> the application of ancestral and local knowledge in the context of dealing with anthropogenic change has been recognised as a key element in national and international climate change policy development. Traditional knowledge informs community understanding of environmental change, use of natural resources and their worldview, all of which play an important role in how communities adapt to climate change. Incorporation of Indigenous knowledge in climate change adaptation strategies can lead to more cost-effective, locally relevant, sustainable approaches being identified, and increased Indigenous ownership and engagement in culturally appropriate adaptation planning processes and outcomes.[40]

If we revisit the parable of the Good Samaritan, we see that a fundamental Christian goal here is restorative justice (*mishpat*). Government and/or giving to Christian aid and advocacy groups isn't about charity in the clichéd or pejorative sense (although charity from a biblical perspective is another way of saying love). Aboriginal peoples have exhibited resilience in the face of natural climate change for the 60,000 years of occupancy. As noted earlier, sea level rose dramatically 8000 years ago in the Torres Strait, and the people have lived as sea farers, dealing with variations in the monsoon and associated naturally forced inundations. Now due to anthropogenic climate change, to which they have contributed next to nothing, Torres Strait Islander peoples require assistance to maintain their human dignity. The strategy places this front and centre. Just as in the parable, there is no hint of paternalism or patronage, just the desire to allow people to be as free as possible from impacts that hinder their flourishing. Surely in a changing climate, this is what good neighbours look like.

Impacts on communities in Northern Australia

The most comprehensive report to date on the impacts of climate change in northern Australia is a 2009 report by the Department of Climate Change and Energy Efficiency.[41] The region includes the Timor Sea and Gulf of Carpentaria river drainage basins, the north-east coastal drainage division north of Cairns, and the Pilbara region of Western Australia. Cities in the study include Darwin, Cairns, Broome, Kununurra, Katherine, Wadeye (Port Keats), Maningrida, Nhulunbuy, Borroloola and Cooktown, and the mining towns of Port Hedland, Karratha, Mt Isa and Weipa.

Aboriginal peoples in northern Australia face many challenges; challenges that will be exacerbated by climate change. Many communities are distant from major transport routes, have minimal communication infrastructure, and lag behind the rest of Australia in indicators relating to health, education, income and employment. Climate change is likely to further impact access to information, goods and services, isolating these communities from participation in market-based economic activity. The report also notes however, that 'relocation of Indigenous people from traditional homelands to the larger regional centres has had a negative impact on their spiritual and social health, as well as reduced opportunities to participate in important cultural activities.'[42] In other words removal for any purpose, including as a climate change mitigation strategy, is fraught with difficulty and highly undesirable.

In terms of climate change scenarios, hot spells (days of temperatures > 35° C) are forecast to increase; the wet season is expected to become wetter while the dry season becomes drier. Sea surface temperatures will increase, and some models suggest that tropical cyclone numbers could decrease, but individual cyclones become more intense. Sea level rise will impact coastal communities. There will likely be a range of impacts on ecosystems that provide Aboriginal people with a food source. Ocean acidification and increasing ocean temperatures will impact coral reefs, rainforests will be more subject to fires, and mangroves, which act as nurseries for fish, are likely to be negatively impacted. The study examines climate change impacts on health, infrastructure, education, and livelihoods. Rather than go through each of these in detail, I will summarise one of the case studies presented, that of Yakanarra.[43]

Yakanarra is an Aboriginal community of about 150 people, located approximately 140 km south of Fitzroy Crossing in the Kimberly region of Western Australia. It is set on one-square mile on Gogo Station, and was established in 1988. The Yakanarra Community Resource Centre states that the 'primary purpose of the Community is to allow indigenous people to practice traditional cultural activities, with a secondary purpose of providing people with a safe and healthy place to live away from town.'[44] There are 30 houses with electricity supplied by diesel powered generators. Ground water is extracted using two electric powered bores. Only a short section of the road between the Great Northern Highway and Yakanarra is bitumen, and most roads are subject to flooding during the wet. As a result, the town can become seasonally isolated. The community normally receives its food supplies by air, and the local strip is capable of landing a Hercules troop transport. Yakanarra is semi-arid country, located in low lying savannah, close to two seasonal creeks that fill during the wet season. The average temperature during the wet is about 40° C. The two weather hazards we will focus on here are the current and expected future impacts of temperature and changes to rainfall.

With temperatures into the 40s, heat is already a major factor in community life. In times of extreme heat, everything slows down. Productivity among adult workers is greatly reduced, and education at the local independent school is also affected. Teaching staff will often take children to a billabong during very hot days. There is sometimes an increase in disputes related to heat stress, which can, at times, turn violent. As an adaptation measure, the basketball court, which provides much needed recreation for the town's youth, is equipped with lights for night activities during the hotter months. As the planet warms, longer periods of above 35° C are expected. An increase in mortality among infants and old people can be expected. During the dry season, an increase in grass fires will limit the community's ability to supplement their food sources with traditional foods such as bush turkey, kangaroo, emu, and yams. Air conditioning and refrigeration facilities will not cope as well with higher temperatures. Power consumption will likely increase, and given that it relies upon diesel generators, the increased demand for electricity could be a drain on community finances.

The wet season has an annual impact on the Yakanarra community. The roads to Yakanarra are regularly cut off as they are mostly unsealed. While the airstrip can support large transport aircraft, the road from the town to the airstrip can also become cut off. Runoff from the bitumen roads increases ponding, leaving rainwater to provide breeding grounds for disease carrying mosquitoes. Some of the bitumen roads are already undercut by floodwater in places and need repair. Flood waters also pose a number of risks in town. There is the possibility, though considered slight by locals, of the sewage evaporation pond flooding into housing. Flood waters could compromise the electric bore pumps and fuel tanks for power and transport. Underground telecommunications can be affected, and a fibre optic cable was severed during floods in 2009. While the community is accustomed to being cut off, and will always welcome 'a good Wet', projected increases in seasonal rainfall will intensify all of the aforementioned impacts. Projected changes in tropical cyclone intensity could increase the risk of catastrophic flooding.

The Yakanarra community is not without its own resources, and its members are resilient and adaptive, with a culture of self-reliance. The community has a strong sense of cohesion, having developed from a camp of rough sheds to a fully developed township with a local council and independent school. Locals say that the community is a 'socially healthy place to live.' During the wet season, most people prefer to stay at Yakanarra rather than relocate to Fitzroy Crossing. The community has an intimate knowledge of the local ecology and connection to the sacred sites. This connection to sacred sites and the Creator Spirit is reflected in both the performance of ceremony, and the sense of responsibility to respect the Creator Spirit in the way in which the land is used. The Yakanarra community have a special affinity with the Kappurtu, a snake-like Creator Spirit associated with water sources. Yakanarra elders perform ceremonies during the build up to each wet season to replenish soak sites, bring the rains, and fill local water sources.

This spiritual framework means that the local peoples interpret unusual weather events and landscape degradation as a lapse in their relationship with the Creator Spirit due to some wrong doing. This belief leads to a spiritual anxiety. Hence, while early warning services and subsequent evacuation can be provided by western science, and impacts on physical health can be mitigated against, as the report warns, 'cultural hazards can only be understood through extended communication with community members themselves.' This highlights the complexity of dealing with the impacts of climate change, and the need for a holistic, multi-levelled approach. As with Torres Strait Islander peoples, relocation can be used as a mitigation strategy, but given the relationship between Aboriginal cultures and land, it is far from satisfactory.

Yakanarra is but one example of remote communities that are being and will be affected by climate change. The 2009 report noted that its study area included some 87,000 people, from 665 settlements of between 50 to 3,500 people. Of these settlements, some 50% of people live within 20 kilometres of the coast or on offshore islands. This means over 40,000 people are at risk from sea level rise, while all will be affected by extreme heat and changes in rainfall.

Colonial carbon

While I will talk more about combating climate change in the last chapter, I wanted to take time to show that the cause of climate change, carbon emissions, is very much a colonial activity. Ronald J Horvath defined colonialism as 'a form of domination – the control by individuals or groups over the territory and/or behavior of other individuals or groups.'[45] In Australia, such domination is seen in the way in which mining rights are granted, and how Aboriginal people's concerns are handled. The proposed Adani Carmichael coal mine in the Galilee basin of Queensland is on the land of the Wangan and Jagalingou people. A 2016 court challenge by senior traditional owner Adrian Burragubba argued that two mining leases that had been approved by the state government extinguished native title. The court did not find in his favour.[46] However, mining leases that clash with native title seem less certain after a ruling by the full bench of the Federal court ruled in favour of a challenge against the Noongar Indigenous land use agreement (ILUA), a deal which would have extinguished native title on 200,000 hectares of land in Western Australia. This was because in the original deal with the WA government, five Noongar applicants had refused to sign on.[47] Rather than accept the wishes of Aboriginal peoples, the Australian government has moved to ensure mining can continue, and made changes to Native Title, with bilateral support.[48]

In the US, the events surrounding the Dakota Access pipeline demonstrate ongoing colonialism. The pipeline will run through the ancestral lands of the Standing Rock Sioux Tribe. The pipeline is an environmental and cultural threat, as pipelines do not have a good safety record.[49] These risks are clearly understood, as an early proposal for the pipeline to run near a white community was rejected on the grounds of risk to water supplies.[50] The move to Sioux land could be interpreted as an act of environmental racism. The Sioux see themselves as water protectors, not protestors. They have attracted widespread support, including from war Veterans, which has led to some moving scenes of reconciliation.[51] In response to the peaceful protests by Sioux and their supporters, authorities have used rubber bullets, pepper spray and water cannons against demonstrators, injuring hundreds.[52] At one point, the North Dakota governor even suggested starving out protestors.[53] President Obama announced in December of 2016 that the pipeline would be rerouted. However, in January of 2017, President Donald Trump signed an executive order that the army corps of engineers was to 'review and approve in an expedited manner' the project.[54] The chairman of the Standing Rock tribe states that this decision disregards tribal interest, and that the whole project has never involved proper consultation with them. This appears to be a common theme in carbon colonialism.

Reconciliation and closing the Gap

Given what we have seen, concrete acts of restorative justice, acts of love towards our Aboriginal and Torres Strait Islander neighbours are required. This applies to Australians and Americans, but UK readers need to remember in both cases these countries were British colonies and there is an historical debt.

In the Australian context, there will be no moving forward until the churches genuinely become involved in the process of Reconciliation. This means non-Indigenous churches listening to our Aboriginal and Torres Strait Islander brothers and sisters about their history, their loss, their dispossession, and their pain. And not only that, but given that Aboriginal peoples lived on this land in a sustainable way for some 60,000 years, and Torres Strait Islander peoples for some 5,000 years, we have much to learn from their wisdom. In an age where climate change is a pressing issue for us all, we need to learn from their wisdom, and join together in action. We have seen above when it comes to Carbon Colonialism in Australia, when we protest against coal mines we don't need, we are supporting climate action, protecting farmland, but also joining in solidarity with Aboriginal peoples.

We also need to educate ourselves. This means educating ourselves as to why such inequality and injustices have arisen in the first place, and organisations like Australians Together (http://www.australianstogether. org.au/) are helpful here. We also need to learn about ourselves as non-

Indigenous Australians. Learning about how white privilege functions without the kneejerk reaction against that term being hopelessly PC will be hard, but it needs to be done. How else can we walk with and love our Aboriginal and Torres Strait Islander neighbours, unless we can come to terms with this?[55] As Gary Foley notes, unless we understand this well, we will be more interested in fulfilling something within ourselves than of seeing justice done.[56]

When it comes to justice issues in general, organisations like TEAR have been working alongside Aboriginal and Torres Strait Islander peoples for many years. At the time of writing, TEAR's programs are undergoing review. For a number of years, the Dhumba program has been the Aboriginal and Torres Strait Islander Support Program of TEAR. Dhumba is a Woi Wurrung word for talk, tell and/or speak. Woi Wurrung is the language of the Wurundjeri people; the traditional custodians of the land on which the TEAR Australia's Melbourne head office is located, and Wurundjeri elders have given their permission for the use of this word. Dhumba captures the aim to build relationships through good communication, listening and talking together. As discussed in the chapter above, *mishpat* in the context of our colonial history must involve listening first. Partnerships are not about repeating the paternalism of the past, but are about relationships for the future. Through Dhumba, TEAR has grown partnerships with Aboriginal and Torres Strait Islander Christian organisations and built further opportunities for community development with Aboriginal and Torres Strait Islander peoples. The focus of the partnerships has been community development training and capacity building. Take for example the Arnhem Human Enterprise Development project to promote wellness in remote Indigenous communities. Nearly half of all adults in remote communities struggle with chronic disease. In the Galiwin'ku community, Dianne Biritjalawuy, Yolngu community leader, has made the journey back from the brink of serious heart disease and uncontrolled diabetes. As Dr Kama Trudgen observes about Dianne's transformation

> Empowered to understand that she could transform her own health, she was then hungry for more information and tools to continue this new way of living. She was supported by AHED with education, cooking

lessons and help to access healthy food options not usually available in her remote community[57]

Dianne's recovery was seen by other community members as evidence that nutrition was powerful and effective. Now there is a crowd funded project run by women who have similarly experienced such healing. They are being catalysts for change in their community.

Another project involved Scripture Union in Rockhampton, QLD. This project involves

Working with local elders and the Darumbal Youth Community Services, the program engages young people with their cultural heritage, understanding the story, song and traditions of their local Mob through cultural games, overnight camping, yarning circles and traditional food. The program takes young people through high energy, risk-taking activities that create numerous opportunities for the young people to challenge their own abilities, build resilience and gain a sense of accomplishment and success. In de-brief sessions, participants reflect on their experiences and their own responses.

Another aspect of Dhumba's work has been raising awareness. As some of my examples from the start show, Christians are not immune from ignorance, misunderstanding and racism. Dhumba has worked with Christians to invite them along the journey with Indigenous Australians, and no doubt TEAR will continue to do so into the future.

Endnotes

1 Nikki Barrowclough, "After the furore, meet the real Adam Goodes," *The Sydney Morning Herald*, 23 January, 2017, accessed 21 February, 2017, http://www.smh.com.au/good-weekend/after-the-furore-meet-the-real-adam-goodes-20160111-gm39aa.html.

2 State Library of Victoria, "Coranderrk Mission," accessed 21 February, 2017, http://ergo.slv.vic.gov.au/explore-history/fight-rights/indigenous-rights/coranderrk-mission.

3 Brad Pillans and L. Keith Fifield, "Erosion rates and weathering history of rock surfaces associated with Aboriginal rock art engravings (petroglyphs) on Burrup Peninsula, Western Australia, from cosmogenic nuclide measurements," *Quaternary Science Reviews* 69 (2013): 98-106.

4 Bill Gammage, *The Biggest Estate on Earth: How Aborigines Made Australia* (Crows Nest, NSW: Allen and Unwin, 2011).

5 Karen Stichtenoth, "Once were eel farmers," *Monash Magazine*, May 2006, accessed 12 February, 2017, http://www.monash.edu.au/pubs/monmag/issue17-2006/research/research-eels.html.

6 Stan Grant, *The Australian Dream: Blood, History and Becoming* (Carlton: Black Inc, 2016).

7 Australian Indigenous Health*Info* Net, "History of Closing the Gap," 15 November, 2016, accessed 12 February, 2017, http://www.healthinfonet.ecu.edu.au/closing-the-gap/key-facts/what-is-the-history-of-closing-the-gap.

8 Oxfam Australia, "Close the Gap," accessed 12 February, 2017, https://www.oxfam.org.au/what-we-do/indigenous-australia/close-the-gap/.

9 Fergus Hunter, 'Closing the Gap: Five numbers that should shame Australia,' *The Sydney Morning Herald*, 10 February, 2016, accessed 12 February, 2017, http://www.smh.com.au/federal-politics/political-news/closing-the-gap-five-numbers-that-should-shame-australia-20160210-gmqlbl.html.

10 Bianca Soldani, "The facts about Indigenous youth detention in Australia," *The Feed*, 26 July, 2016, accessed 28 May, 2017, http://www.sbs.com.au/news/thefeed/article/2016/07/26/facts-about-indigenous-youth-detention-australia.

11 Siobhan Fogarty, "Suicide rate for young Indigenous men highest in world, Australian report finds," *ABC News*, 12 August, 2016, accessed 3 June, 2017, http://www.abc.net.au/news/2016-08-12/indigenous-youth-suicide-rate-highest-in-world-report-shows/7722112.

12 Midnight Oil, *Beds are burning*

13 Graham Paulson, and Mark Brett, "Five Smooth Stones: Reading the Bible through Aboriginal Eyes, "*Colloquium*, 45 (2013): 199-209.

14 Djinijini Gondarra, "Aboriginal and Christian – Developing an Indigenous Theology," *National Outlook*, February, 1984.

15 Rainbow Spirit Elders, *Rainbow Spirit Theology: Towards an Australian Theology Second Edition* (Hindmarsh SA: ATF Press, 2007), 59.

16 Australian Catholic Social Justice Council, *Jubilee justice: a statement for Social Justice Sunday 1999 from the Catholic Bishops of Australia* (North Sydney: Australian Catholic Social Justice Council, 1999).

17 Peter Adam, "Australia-whose land? A call for recompense: John Sanders Lecture 2009," 11 August, 2009, accessed 18 may, 2017, https://www.ridley.edu.au/resource/australia-whose-land-christian-call-recompense/.

18 Ray Minniecon, "A letter from Pastor Ray Minniecon," *Indigenous Hospitality House Newsletter*, May 2012, accessed 31 May, 2017, http://www.brunswick.unitingchurch.org.au/newspdfs/Indigenous%20Hospitality%20House%20May.pdf.

19 Edwards, *Sin and Salvation in the South Land of the Holy Spirit*, in Discovering an Australian Theology, ed. Peter Malone (Homebush: St Paul Publications, 1988), 91.

20 Alfred A. Cave, "Canaanites in a Promised Land: The American Indian and the Providential Theory of Empire," *American Indian Quarterly*, 12 (1988): 277-297.

21 Mark Brett, "Reconciliation and Indigenous Rights: What Churches Can Learn from Roger Williams," ABC Religion and Ethics, 27 May, 2016, accessed 11 February, 2017, http://www.abc.net.au/religion/articles/2016/05/27/4470813.htm.

22 Peter Lewis, "Acting in Solidarity? A Theological Understanding of the Church's

Journey with Indigenous Peoples in Australia." *A paper for presentation at the Australian Missiology Conference, Melbourne, 26 to 30 September 2005*, accessed 10 February, 2017, https://groupsthatclick.com/files/missiolconf/Papers/Lewis.pdf.

23 NASA, 'Global Climate Change: Vital Signs of the Planet: Sea Level Rise,' September 2016, accessed 7 February, 2017, http://climate.nasa.gov/vital-signs/sea-level/.

24 IPCC, 2013, *Summary for Policymakers. In: Climate Change 2013: The Physical Science Basis. Contribution of Working Group I to the Fifth Assessment Report of the Intergovernmental Panel on Climate Change* [Stocker, T.F., D. Qin, G.-K. Plattner, M. Tignor, S.K. Allen, J. Boschung, A. Nauels, Y. Xia, V. Bex and P.M. Midgley (eds.)]. Cambridge University Press, Cambridge, United Kingdom and New York, NY, USA, 23.

25 Nicola Jones, "Abrupt sea Level rise looms as increasingly realistic threat," *Yale Environment 360*, May 5, 2016, accessed 7 February, 2017, http://e360.yale.edu/features/abrupt_sea_level_rise_realistic_greenland_antarctica.

26 David Archer and Victor Brovkin, "The Millennial Atmospheric Lifetime of Anthropogenic CO_2," *Climatic Change* 90 (2008): 283-297.

27 Torres Strait Regional Authority, "The Torres Strait General History," accessed 7 February, 2017, http://www.tsra.gov.au/the-torres-strait/general-history.

28 Saila Huusko, "We're sinking here: Climate change laps at front door of Torres Strait Islands," *The Guardian*, 8 December, 2016, accessed 6 February, 2017, https://www.theguardian.com/australia-news/2015/dec/08/were-sinking-here-climate-change-laps-at-front-door-of-torres-strait-islands.

29 Ross Garnaut, "The Eddie Koiki Mabo Lecture 2009: Climate Change from the Perspective of the Torres Strait," accessed 7 February, 2017, https://www.jcu.edu.au/__data/assets/pdf_file/0013/122404/jcu_145040.pdf.

30 Ramasamy Suppiah, Janice Bathols, Mark Collier, David Kent and Julian O'Grady, *Observed and Future Climates of the Torres Strait* (Aspendale: CSIRO, 2010).

31 Saila Huusko, *We're sinking here.*

32 TSRA (2014), *Torres Strait Climate Change Strategy 2014–2018. Report prepared by the Land and Sea Management Unit*, Torres Strait Regional Authority, July 2014, 36p.

33 Elaine Kelly, "Rising seas pose a cultural threat to Australia's 'Forgotten People'," *The Conversation*, 27 November, 2014, accessed 6 February, 2017, http://theconversation.com/rising-seas-pose-a-cultural-threat-to-australias-forgotten-people-34359.

34 Climate Council of Australia Limited, "Climate Council Alert: Climate change and coral bleaching," 3 February, 2016, accessed 7 February, 2017, https://www.climatecouncil.org.au/climate-change-coral-bleaching.

35 Nance Huxton, "Calls for detailed climate change plan for Torres Strait Islands amid projected sea level rises," *ABC News,* 5 January, 2015, accessed 7 February, 2017, http://www.abc.net.au/news/2015-01-05/call-for-torres-strait-climate-change-plan/6000646.

36 Salia Huusko, *We're sinking here.*

37 Elaine Kelley, *Rising seas.*

38 Glenn Albrecht, "The age of solastalgia," *The Conversation,* 7 August, 2012, accessed

3 June, 2017, https://theconversation.com/the-age-of-solastalgia-8337.

39 TSRA (2014), *Torres Strait Climate Change Strategy*, 18.

40 TSRA (2014), *Torres Strait Climate Change Strategy*, 20.

41 Green D, S Jackson and J Morrison, 2009, *Risks from Climate Change to Indigenous Communities in the Tropical North of Australia*. Department of Climate Change and Energy Efficiency: Canberra.

42 Green, Jackson and Morrison, *Risks from Climate Change*, 16.

43 Green, Jackson and Morrison, *Risks from Climate Change*, 84-91.

44 Yakanarra Community Resource Centre, "Our Community: Our Shire," accessed 9 February, 2017, http://www.yakanarra.crc.net.au/OurCommunity/OurShire/Pages/default.aspx.

45 Ronald J. Horvath, "A Definition of Colonialism," *Current Anthropology*, 13 (1972):45-57.

46 Andrew Kos, "Indigenous challenge to Adani Carmichael coal mine dismissed by Federal Court," *ABC News*, 19 August, 2016, accessed 3 March, 2017, http://www.abc.net.au/news/2016-08-19/indigenous-challenge-to-adani-carmichael-coal-mine-dismissed/7765466.

47 Helen Davidson, "Adani mine leases and national parks in doubt after native title court decision," *The Guardian*, 5 February, 2017, accessed 3 March, 2017, https://www.theguardian.com/australia-news/2017/feb/05/adani-mine-leases-and-national-parks-in-doubt-after-native-title-court-decision.

48 Joshua Robertson, "Coalition to change native title laws to protect mining and agriculture deals," *The Guardian*, 13 February, 2017, accessed 3 March, 2017, https://www.theguardian.com/australia-news/2017/feb/13/coalition-to-change-native-title-laws-to-protect-mining-and-agriculture-deals; Joe Kelly, and Michael McKenna, "Native title changes crucial to Adani coalmine pass through the Senate," *The Australian*, 15 June, 2017, accessed 17 June, 2017, http://www.theaustralian.com.au/national-affairs/indigenous/native-title-changes-crucial-to-adani-coalmine-pass-through-the-senate/news-story/729d4bd43b5c8d464bbd94255dc0236a.

49 Bec Crew, "The thing the Standing Rock Protestors were afraid of just happened," *Science Alert*, December 14, 2016, accessed December 18, 2016, http://www.sciencealert.com/that-thing-the-standing-rock-protesters-were-afraid-of-just-happened.

50 Amy Dalrymple, "Pipeline route plan first called for crossing north of Bismarck," *Bismarck Tribune*, August 18, 2016, accessed December 18, 2016, http://bismarcktribune.com/news/state-and-regional/pipeline-route-plan-first-called-for-crossing-north-of-bismarck/article_64d053e4-8a1a-5198-a1dd-498d386c933c.html.

51 Sandy Tolan, "Veterans came to North Dakota to protest a pipeline. But they also found healing and forgiveness," *Los Angeles Times*, December 17, 2016, accessed December 18, 2016, http://www.latimes.com/nation/la-na-north-dakota-20161210-story.html. Accessed 18/12/2016.

52 Jack Healy, "North Dakota Oil Pipeline Battle: Who's fighting and why?" *New York Times*, August 26, 2016, accessed December 18, 2016, http://www.nytimes.com/2016/11/02/us/north-dakota-oil-pipeline-battle-whos-fighting-and-why.html.

53 Josh Voorhees, "North Dakota police want to deny Standing Rock protestors food and shelter," *Slate*, November 29, 1016, accessed December 18, 2016, http://www.slate.com/blogs/the_slatest/2016/11/29/_north_dakota_police_will_cut_off_standing_rock_protesters_supplies.html. Terry Sylvester, "Standing Rock protesters won't be blockaded as North Dakota back down," *Huffington Post*, November 29, 2016, accessed December 19, 2016, http://www.huffingtonpost.com/entry/standing-rock-protest-blockade_us_583df645e4b0c33c8e12ad8e.

54 Oliver Milman, "Standing Rock Sioux tribe says Trump is breaking law with Dakota Access order," *The Guardian*, 27 January, 2017, accessed 3 March, 2017, https://www.theguardian.com/us-news/2017/jan/26/standing-rock-sioux-tribe-trump-breaking-law-dakota-access.

55 For a US perspective on white privilege and culture that makes a similar point, see Ijeoma Oluo, "White People: I Don't Want You To Understand Me Better, I Want You To Understand Yourselves," *The Establishment*, 7 February, 2017, accessed 3 June, 2017, https://theestablishment.co/white-people-i-dont-want-you-to-understand-me-better-i-want-you-to-understand-yourselves-a6fbedd42ddf.

56 The Juice Media, "Gary Foley: Advice for white Indigenous activists in Australia," Filmed [31 August, 2010]. YouTube video, 03:09. Posted [5 September, 2010]. https://www.youtube.com/watch?v=uEGsBV9VGTQ.

57 Kama Trudgen, "Nurturing Wellness in Remote Indigenous Communities," *TEAR Australia*, accessed 12 March, 2017, http://www.tear.org.au/projects/nurturing-wellness-in-remote-indigenous-communities.

Chapter 6 — Shaking the pillars

Merry Christmas Mr Abbott

I like Christmas presents. I enjoy getting them. I also rather like giving them. So in 2015, when the Christian lobby group Common Grace were asking for donations to buy solar panels for Kirribilli House, the Sydney residence of the Prime Minister of Australia, I was tickled by the idea. The Prime Minister at the time, Tony Abbott, had declared in 2009 that climate change was crap.[1] His policies on climate change were rather lukewarm to say the least: repealing the price on carbon that the previous government had instituted, and abolishing the Climate Commission. Thankfully, the Climate Commission has risen like a phoenix from the ashes to become the Climate Council, a crowd funded body. Just recently, the Climate Institute, a climate change-focused think-tank and lobby group shut its doors due to lack of funding.[2]

So it was rather unsurprising when the Prime Minister rejected our Christmas present. The excuse was predictably weak; that there would be ongoing requirement for cleaning and maintenance of the panels. The Australian Solar Council told Jody Lightfoot of Common Grace that 'panels do not require annual cleaning and maintenance; they are cleaned by the rain.'[3] Instead, Lightfoot opined that 'the rejection of the solar panels is symbolic of the government's failure to invest in renewable energy when 89 per cent of Australians want a stronger renewable energy target.' So given the gift was refused, the targets are still weak and little appears to have changed, was this little more than a stunt? Or does it represent an action by people seeking to be good neighbours to those we have been talking about in the past few chapters? It's time to look at the parable with fresh eyes to answer this question.

Reading parables

By now you will be familiar with the idea that I have been developing of a connection between many of the justice issues that concern Christians, and climate change. By altering the climate, we affect the ecosystems upon which we all depend. We affect our agricultural systems that force people into poverty, displacement, and sometimes put them at greater risk of being trafficked. Women are particularly at risk. Sometimes displacement leads to violence and internal conflict. Displacement can come in the form of external migration, and we are seeing more borders being closed. The sum of this is that it makes sense that Sustainable Development Goal 13 is action on climate, because it affects all of the other goals.

We have looked at the idea of justice as restoration; the Hebrew word for this is *mishpat*. All human being are made in the image of God, and hence have what has come to be called human rights. We might argue over exactly what to call it, we might disagree with other beliefs about the exact nature of their basis. However, human beings responding as image bearers of God who sees another in need, want to respond in a helpful manner. The idea of *mishpat* does not reduce justice to being in love with the idea itself, but being moved by *hesed*, a faithful love, and by a humility before God, we seek to lift others up (Micah 6:8). Like the Good Samaritan, we pay the cost to restore people to wholeness, producing a flourishing human being, not a victim or a dependent.

There is another idea in Hebrew that discusses justice, but before we meet it, we need to return to the parable. Everyone wants to identify with the Good Samaritan, but we saw that this actually involves cost. There is the material cost of money and resources, in order to see people restored. It can also be time-consuming. The Samaritan goes out of his way to bring the victim of violence to a place of rest, using his own bandages, oil and wine. He goes away and leaves the man in the care of the innkeeper. In this sense, doing justice is a team effort. There's no better way to burn yourself out than trying to go it alone, all the more so when we forget it is because we love God, or indeed because God first loved us, that we can do justice. What is more, the Samaritan promises to return. Justice is not something you do on a short-term mission trip; justice is a lifetime commitment to doing what is just.

So everyone wants to be known as the Good Samaritan, but we can be the Good Innkeeper as well. Hopefully none of us wants to be the priest or Levite. Not that they were bad people per se, but we can see in the traditional understanding of the text that they put religious formalism above love; orthodoxy above orthopraxy. None of this is to say you need to be a 'progressive' Christian in order to be involved in justice. Sometimes we can get caught up in labels in an unhelpful manner. I identify as Evangelical, but sometimes use other terms to make it clear what I mean by this. Ultimately, what the parable is calling us to be is God and neighbour lovers, and given it is Jesus telling us to do this, followers of him as well.

However, before going back to the priest and Levite, it is worth asking is there anyone else in the parable we have failed to talk about? It turns out the most often neglected characters in this story are the robbers, or more correctly, bandits. In order to understand the parable fully, we need to understand them and their backstory. In doing this, I realise that I am going beyond the immediate point of the parable. Typically when you pick up a book that looks at the parables, you'll read that there is only one main point to most, if not all parables. You are warned to not look too deeply into some of the incidental details of the parable. Sometimes you might get a discussion of what the church did with parables in the Middle Ages as a warning. All of this is fair and useful to enable the reader to engage in *exegesis*, reading from the text, rather than *eisegesis*, reading into the text. However, I think what I am about to do enlarges the meaning of the parable precisely because, in giving the historical details of the world behind the text, we can understand each of the characters more. This reading will amplify our understanding of justice, not diminish it.

A very naughty boy

You might be familiar with the Monty Python movie, *The Life of Brian*. Now I realise this is a problematic movie for some Christians. Indeed, if you look carefully at all Python humour, you will see a strong absurdist streak than can only come from an atheistic worldview. John Cleese, a member of the Python crew, can be a very staunch and outspoken atheist. I once watched a documentary about the making of *The Life of Brian* and the reactions it received. The Python crew claimed that they found Jesus admirable, and couldn't bring themselves to make fun of him. However, what they did do in the movie was make fun of religion itself, and to a degree I think that can be a helpful thing. There is much about the modern Church that deserves ridicule. However, while we might join in a little on this fun, the song *Always look on the bright side of life* reflects on the absurdity of life in a godless universe. This isn't something a Christian can really sing along to. But there is one scene I want us to reflect on.

The main protagonist of the movie is Brian, who ends up being mistaken for a Messianic pretender, a wannabe revolutionary. Angry at Roman occupation he joins the revolutionary Judean People's Front. There is a comic dialogue where their leader fulminates against the Roman Empire, 'what has Rome ever done for us?' he asks. In response, members of the group provide a long list of things that Rome brought to the world, like roads, a postal service, aqueducts, and so on. But while Roman colonies received these benefits, Rome brought a much more sinister influence into the world.

Rome brought peace to the world, the so-called *Pax Romana* (Roman Peace), but it did so through military conquest. The peace was maintained through violence, where dissent and resistance was crushed with ruthless efficiency.[4] Professor of Classics John Richardson suggests that warfare and conquest was the principle activity that occupied the Roman senate and was the main focus of their foreign policy.[5] Furthermore, Roman historian J. A. North makes four points that indicate that Roman warfare was deliberately aggressive:

1. Both the expectations and the social ethos of Romans of high and low status were geared to regular war-making; they had the attitudes and habits which go with this way of life.

2. Many Romans, including all those who had a major influence on policy decisions, made, and knew they made, large profits out of warfare and out of the expansion of the Empire.

3. Expansion was a publicly stated aim, uninhibited by the laws that covered treaties. Treaties were made to be broken.

4. Roman wars were often aggressive in intention, even if not formally so.[6]

The link with profit is an interesting one. In *Colossians Remixed: Subverting the Empire*, Walsh and Keesmaat define empire as

... totalising by definition. In the words of the Psalmist, imperial 'mouths lay claim to heaven, and their tongues take possession of the earth' (Ps 73:9 NIV). Empires are built on systematic centralizations of power and secured by structures of socio-economic and military control. They are religiously legitimated by powerful myths that are rooted in foundational assumptions, and they are sustained by a proliferation of imperial symbols that capture the imagination of the populace.[7]

There is a link between military and economic control. Professor of ancient history Keith Hopkins suggests that the Roman Empire was split into a threefold military and taxation structure.[8] Firstly, there was the outer ring of frontier provinces in which defensive armies were stationed. Secondly, there was the inner ring of relatively rich tax-exporting provinces, such as Spain, southern Gaul, northern Africa, Asia Minor, Syria and Egypt. Finally, Rome was the seat of the central government which, like the armies, consumed a large volume of taxes. By and large, this meant that Rome lived in luxury while the rest of the empire lived in relative or actual poverty. Heavy taxation often resulted in farmers losing their land and becoming peasant tenant farmers.[9] At the same time, Hopkins suggests that heavy taxation increased trade within the empire.[10] In order to pay the taxes, local farmers had to sell some of their food surplus locally, which was consumed by local artisans or exported to other parts of the empire. Some of the goods of the artisans made were used locally, others exported. The largest consumer of goods was Rome itself and the frontier armies, who consumed more goods than taxes that were collected locally. Hence, Hopkins comments that:

the model implies an increased monetization of the Roman economy, the commercialization of exchange, an elongation of the links between producers and consumers, the growth of specialist intermediaries (traders, shippers, bankers), and an unprecedented level of urbanization. The model illustrates the close connection between changes on the level of individual action by simple peasants and relatively large-scale changes, such as the growth of towns.[11]

Local economies were disrupted as reserves were plundered, skilled and unskilled labour was enslaved and loans with high rates of interest led to a loss of land ownership.

These taxes were collected by tax collectors of course, and you'll be familiar with them from the New Testament. They were not very popular figures. Matthew Levi was one, but he abandoned his profiteering to follow Jesus (Mark 2:14). Zacchaeus was a chief tax collector, who underwent a dramatic turnaround (Luke 19:1-10). Tax collectors were not the sort of people that the religiously minded spent time with (Matthew 9:9-11). This was because the tax that these tax collectors took was for Rome, and this made tax collectors collaborators with the oppressive pagan regime. However, as we noted earlier, there was also a temple tax to pay (e.g. Matthew 17:24-27). This tax could also be onerous on the poor (Mark 12:38-44). This temple tax went toward supporting the priests and Levites. You can begin to see why perhaps the priest and Levite in the parable didn't stop purely for reasons of ritual purity, but more of that in a moment.

Robbing hood

So we can now turn to the bandits in the parable of the Good Samaritan. Sometimes the word is translated as robbers or thieves, but this is inadequate. In Greek the word *kleptes* means thief, and from it we get the word in English, kleptomaniac, which refers to a compulsive thief. Thieves like this were sneaky, but not often violent. For example, in Luke 12:39 we read that Jesus will return like a thief in the night, that is unexpectedly. The word used in Luke 10 is *lestai*, and this means more than a mere thief. In the world of first-century Palestine, the word *lestai* could either refer to highwaymen who robbed for personal gain, or guerrilla fighters who targeted Roman authorities and their Jewish collaborators. The Jewish historian Josephus uses *lestai* to refer to Jewish social banditry, a form of primitive rebellion often found under oppressive situations such as Jewish life under Roman rule.[12] These conditions were usually viewed as unjust by the common people as well.[13] We might compare the *lestai* to Robin Hood, for bandits could 'enjoy the support of their village or of the people in general and they have no difficulty rejoining their community periodically or permanently.'[14]

The oppressive conditions under which banditry flourished have already been touched upon, such as taxation and foreign rule. The

Roman taxation system consisted of direct taxes, levied against agricultural products, and indirect taxes in the form of custom dues, road tolls, and market taxes. Add to that a client or vassal rulership, where the Sadducees and Herodians collaborated with Rome, and the High Priest was a puppet figure chosen directly by Rome. So oppressive was taxation under Herod the Great that after his death a deputation was sent to Rome to void his will giving rule to his three sons, presumably because the taxation regime would continue to be as severe. Herod's building program, including that of second temple, was funded by heavy taxation.

The Jewish aristocracy benefitted from the temple tax, which supported their comfortable lifestyle. This tax also supported the ordinary priest. Furthermore, severe taxation could leave the ordinary Israelite landless, and it was often the aristocracy who bought up land to form large estates. The landless Israelite could become an itinerant day worker, as we read about in many of Jesus' parables, or they could become *lestai*. We can now see that while the motivation of the priest and Levite could have been in part a concern for ritual purity, given their complicity in a system that many ordinary people found oppressive, they were in a hurry not to themselves become victim to such violence.

So how does this broader context help us unpack the parable for our modern situation?

Fossil fool empires

We've seen that the *lestai* were a reaction to an unjust system. While they turned to violence to protest against it, there were those embedded in the Empire who were doing very well out of the situation; the Emperor, the Roman senate, and the rich families of Rome. The rest of the world fed their lifestyle and the military system that protected it. We need to think about where we sit in the story, but for most of you, these are not the background characters to identify with. I'll get to us in a minute. And yes, I know the dangers of pointing the finger of blame at others. In the Gulag Archipelago, Aleksandr Solzhenitsyn warns us

> If only there were evil people somewhere insidiously committing evil deeds, and it were necessary only to separate them from the rest of us

and destroy them. But the line dividing good and evil cuts through the heart of every human being. And who is willing to destroy a piece of his own heart?[15]

However, it is important for the church to speak prophetically, as I'll discuss more below. We need to be able to speak truth to power and identify injustice, yet humbly and non-violently. In this sense, unlike the *lestai*, we will occupy the Badlands as sacred spaces, the margins where the non-violent kingdom is breaking in.[16]

The first group to identify is the fossil fuel industry. Let's be honest at this point. The fossil fuel industry (and some might argue the politicians who promote their cause and then retire from politics to work in that same industry) can be identified as modern Caesars, senators, and the rich families of Rome. It would be fair to say that society has benefitted enormously from fossil fuels. The point is not that great good has not been achieved; think about the value of transport, lighting, heating and cooking that we all take for granted, while many in the world still have to use solid fuels with the attendant fire risks and air quality issues. According to a 2011 study for example, some three billion people use biomass and coal as their primary method of heating and cooking. A WHO report from 2002 estimates that indoor smoke from solid fuels may be responsible for about 1.6 million premature deaths.[17] But climate change shows us that there are limits to the burning of fossil fuels; it's time to stop and yet the industry doesn't want us to. This was abundantly clear when it was revealed that oil and gas company Santos had adopted a business strategy consistent with 4° C of warming.[18] This would be catastrophic!

The science of greenhouse gases absorbing and retaining heat in the atmosphere is over 150 years old. We now know that the fossil fuel giant Exxon has known for over 30 years that its industry has been warming the planet. Rather than change their business model, or simply keep quiet, Exxon has actively promoted misinformation. Exxon has funded 'advertorials' declaring the science was uncertain. CEO Rex Tillerson consistently played doubt on the science, and even now while declaring the impact will be great, says 'the people of the world will not – and should not – give up refrigerators and cars and increasing standards of living.'[19] In other words, keep using fossil fuels. Denial goes back to 1997 where the then CEO Lee 'Iron Ass' Raymond said that computer models were 'notoriously inaccurate.' Yet while many details in the models have changed, the fundamental story has not changed over many years.[20] Exxon has known this. They were taking carbon dioxide measurements at sea back in 1979, and started building their own climate models in 1982. Exxon scientists have published more than 50 peer-reviewed papers on climate change, and Exxon even funded a research group at MIT with US$3.8 million over 19 years. Over roughly the same period however, they funded sceptics to the tune of US$31 billion.[21]

Likewise, the Australian political system has continued to promote fossil fuel use. Australia experienced a massive heatwave during February of 2017. On the 11th of February, most of New South Wales experienced temperatures at least 12° C warmer than average. The record for the state's highest overnight temperature, 34.2° C, was set in White Cliffs. Meanwhile, Mungindi on the NSW and Queensland border broke the Australia record with 50 days in a row of maximum temperatures over 35° C. Based on computer models which compare modern and pre-industrial atmospheric CO_2 concentrations, heat waves this bad are now twice as likely to occur due to human influence.[22] While all of this was going on, and NSW faced the threat of power black outs, Australian treasurer Scott Morrison was passing around a lump of coal, jokingly assuring us coal is not dangerous. Conservative politicians used power blackouts in the state of South Australia as an opportunity to denigrate renewable energy.[23] Of course, the black outs had nothing to do with renewable energy, as states with little renewable energy also risked blackouts. Only consumer action averted a blackout in New South Wales.[24] It is possible that rooftop solar also played a role.[25] Prime Minister Malcolm Turnbull is planning to change rules governing the Clean Energy Finance Corporation (CEFC) to spend money set aside for renewable energy on so-called clean coal technology, carbon capture and storage.[26] Globally there has been very little to show for all of the investment in clean coal technology, and it would be more expensive than renewable energy.[27] It is very clear that the burning of fossil fuels is increasing the incidence of heat waves, and that most of our remaining fossil fuels need to stay in the ground.[28]

As I write, in the United States the head of the Environmental Protection Agency (EPA), Scott Pruitt says about carbon dioxide that 'I would not agree that it's a primary contributor to the global warming that we see.' This runs counter to the EPA's own website which says 'Carbon dioxide is the primary greenhouse gas that is contributing to recent climate change.'[29] Of course, it runs counter to the scientific consensus of bodies like NASA, NOAA, the Australian Bureau of Meteorology, in fact any climate science research centre or national weather service you can think of. Pruitt has a history of aggression toward the EPA, and has sued it 14 times. It has recently been uncovered that Pruitt has had close links with oil and gas producers, electricity utilities and conservative political groups with ties to the libertarian billionaire Koch brothers. As attorney general of Oklahoma, Pruitt attempted to roll back environmental regulations.[30] While politicians continue to 'get into bed with' big energy, meaningful action on climate change will remain difficult to achieve.

Mirror, mirror on the wall, who's the biggest bandit of them all?

But what about us, those of us not involved directly in polluting industries or failing to make the right policy decisions? As hard as it might be to hear, I think we can identify closely with the bandits, the *lestai*. Given that the *lestai* were under Roman rule, they are victims as well as perpetrators. As victims, they are fellow sufferers under a system designed to make money for the few rather than the many. Today, we hear talk of the 1% of the global population owning as much wealth as the other 99%.[31] A 2017 report states that the eight richest billionaires have as much wealth as the poorest 50% of the global population. Of the 103 countries in the report, 51% have had their inclusive development index scores decline over the past five years, indicating that societies around the world are becoming increasingly unequal.[32]

As perpetrators, the *lestai* point in the exact opposite direction to that which a Christian should be heading. Jesus was crucified with two *lestai* (Mark 15:27), whom Luke 23:39 describes as criminals. These men and Jesus were under the same condemnation, as one of them berated to the other (Luke 23:40). It is also telling that Barabbas was released, one who was guilty of murder in an insurrection (Luke 23:19). It is likely that Jesus took Barabbas' place among his colleagues, which is why one of them could point out that Jesus was innocent, had not been involved in any recent violent revolution, and therefore did not deserve the sentence of crucifixion (Luke 23:41). Barabbas himself is described as a *lestes* (singular of *lestai*) in John 18:40. And so, given what we know about how they were viewed by the general populace, we can understand why they might have favoured him over Jesus.[33]

So let's think about the bandits and us. As victims under the system that has damaged the climate, we have businesses that lie (e.g. Exxon), think tanks that lie (any funded by the Koch brothers), politicians that lie, and not many environmentally friendly products or renewable energy sources to fuel our lives. And yet as perpetrators, as we consume, ignore our impact on the climate, and hence impact the global poor and future generations, we are the bandits. Just as first century bandits had the choice to choose non-violent taking up of the cross over violence (Mark 8:34), resistance and dissent over consent and obedience, so do we. Christians in the developed world wield power, and it is a power we need to use. So if we are part of the system, regardless of who we identify with in the parable, what does that mean for justice? It is now that we turn to another word in the bible. In Jeremiah 9:23-24 we read

Thus says the LORD: Do not let the wise boast in their wisdom, do not let the mighty boast in their might, do not let the wealthy boast in their wealth; but let those who boast boast in this, that they understand and know me, that I am the LORD; I act with steadfast love, justice, and *righteousness* in the earth, for in these things I delight, says the LORD (emphasis mine). (NASB)

In my life I find people tell me that I tend to be too self-depreciating, and at other times I have been accused of being arrogant. Walking the right line can be hard. Humility as a virtue is taken for granted in the church, even if it is not always practiced. It is not without reason that pride is one of the seven deadly sins. Yet this passage tells us to boast! We might think that we are wise in our understanding of justice and the many complex issues involved, but we are not to boast in that. And we might have big wallets to give to every cause that captures our hearts. It costs so little to sponsor a child, for example, and make a big difference in their lives. Yet we are not to boast in that either! No, we are to boast in the fact that we know the Lord.

So what does this mean? J I Packer thought that the idea of knowing God was so important that he wrote a book with that title. We are told here to boast that we know and understand the Lord. Not just God in the abstract, but the covenant name of the God of Abraham, Isaac, and Jacob, and ultimately the Father of Jesus Christ as we come to know in the New Testament. In this passage from Jeremiah 9 we see two old friends. Steadfast love (*hesed*) is God's covenant love. God doesn't give up on us even if we give up on God; God is true to God's promises. We see this time and time again throughout the Old Testament, and in a time of ecological disaster we hope that it is still true. The other is *mishpat*; this idea of restorative justice. God restores the fortune of the poor, widow, fatherless and alien.

The third word here, translated as righteousness is the Hebrew word *tzadeqah* (pronounced tsade'ka). This is different to restorative justice, as Tim Keller comments:

> ... in the Bible, *tzadeqah* refers to day-to-day living in which a person conducts all relationships in family and society with fairness, generosity and equity. ... *tzadeqah*, is behavior that, if it was prevalent in the world, would render rectifying justice unnecessary, because everyone would be living in right relationship to everyone else. Therefore, though *tzadeqah* is primarily about being in a right relationship with God, the righteous life that results is profoundly social.

So what does this mean in terms of climate change and the global poor? It means that as bandits, we have lived under the present system for a long time, and owe an ecological debt to those who suffer the most, yet have contributed to the problem the least. We not only need to do acts of restorative justice (*mishpat*), but we also need to repent. We need to be righteous and do righteousness towards the creation and the poor. And we need to take action to challenge and change the system from within. Climate change affects all of the justice issues that the church concerns itself with, and climate change results from not being in right relationship with God, and hence with each other and the creation in which we live.

There are some biblical examples which illustrate this nicely. Like Moses, we need to use our status for the benefit of others. Moses was adopted by the Pharaoh as his son, raised and educated by the royal household, and after running away, returned to use his access to the royal court to plead with the Pharaoh to let his people go. I'm not sure if any ordinary Israelite could have just walked up and asked to speak to the Pharaoh, who was to the Egyptians the image of God. Another example was Queen Esther. Quite explicitly we read that 'And who knows whether you have not attained royalty for such a time as this? (Esther 4:14, NASB).' For all our seeming powerlessness, we get to vote for government. Despite the power of business and mining groups, our voices are still heard. Despite attempts to limit them, we have the right to protest. At a time when Western powers still have the opportunity to lead the world in the right direction on climate, ordinary Christians, Christian activists, theologians, climate scientists, politicians and others have attained our position for a time such as this.

I also think the example of Zacchaeus is helpful (Luke 19:1-10). As a chief tax collector, he would have farmed out the collection of taxes to others. He was at the centre of the local hub of the system, making a good living by taking money off the top of what was collected. Despised by his countrymen, Zacchaeus was a collaborator with Rome, but an encounter with Jesus turned all of that around. His repentance was dramatic; half of what he owned would go to the poor. We do not read that Jesus asked him to do this, but instead it was his personal conviction of what was the right thing to do. We can compare him with the unnamed rich ruler (Luke 18:18-30) who was called to sell everything and give it away, but couldn't. In the end, the amount of money is less of an issue than the attitude behind it. Zacchaeus' ill-gotten gains would be spent well. A modern example might be the Bill Gates Foundation, where profits from questionable Microsoft business practices are being used for positive ends in healthcare and education.[34]

Furthermore, we read in Luke 19:8 that Zacchaeus also declared 'and if I have defrauded anyone of anything, I will give back four times as much.' The 'if' is not a conditional statement; of course he had defrauded people. Zacchaeus promise exceeds the 20% that Leviticus 6:2-5 calls for. The principle is clear: if one has defrauded someone, following some letter of the law is insufficient to atone for the grievance. Given western countries have profited more and for longer from burning fossil fuels, and have added more than their fair share of greenhouse gases to the atmosphere than the global poor who suffer more, our ecological debt is huge. How can we rightly refuse to be generous in response with funds for adaptation and mitigation of climate change? As we are part of this financial system, or at least have a say in how tax is collected and used, we, like Zacchaeus, must be generous and call for generosity. This of course was the whole point of chapter two. So now let's look at some examples of engaging the powers; how to be a Moses, an Esther, or a Zacchaeus.

Engaging the powers
Campaigning for climate justice

Advocacy on climate change issues has become part of the regular practice of a number of Christian aid, development, and advocacy groups. One of the most recent campaigns is Renew Our World. Jo Knight, the National Advocacy Coordinator of TEAR Australia explains:

Renew Our World is spurring a movement of Christians to become active global citizens who long to see God's world renewed. We believe we need to shift our thinking, our behaviour and our policies to build a restorative economy–an economy based on biblical principles that are just and sustainable. In our prayers, and through our actions, together we are shaping a world that reflects God's love for all creation so that all people can enjoy fullness of life. Our first campaign focus is the critical issue of climate change and its impacts on people in poverty who are hit first and hardest.

TEAR Australia is proud to be co-creating Renew Our World with other Christian organisations from the global north and south such as Tearfund, Micah global, Anglican Alliance, EU-CORD and EFICOR.

There are few genuine climate sceptics in the developing world, because people in poverty can directly see the impacts. People like Sylvia, a mother of four from the village of Chirambi in Malawi, struggle to bridge the 'hunger gap', the time between eating the last of one year's harvest and picking the next. Sylvia has observed that 'when I was a girl, the rains used to come consistently, and it was good for farming. But last year, I harvested four bags of maize from my garden, and I only have one bag left. In the past, I needed 20 bags to feed my children and elderly mother.'[35]

Because of stories like this, the Renew Our World campaign is designed to place pressure on governments to make good on promises made in the Paris Agreement. This is becoming more difficult as America has withdrawn from the agreement, but this is all the more reason for Christians to raise their voices in prayer and advocacy.[36]

The underpinning idea behind Renew Our World is the restorative economy.[37] The restorative economy recognises the paradox that 'the more we succeed in economic development, the more we fail on environmental sustainability.'[38] Agencies like TEAR, Tearfund, Micah, etc. are seeing the impacts worldwide of unsustainable economic practices, like overuse of water. Global inequality is also a major issue, where the world's poorest are kept there by inequality in purchasing and political power.

Instead of relying upon changes in inertia, heavy systems like politics, the restorative economy, and hence the Renew Our World campaign, calls for a different story to the present economic narrative. The narrative is that of Jubilee, which we discussed in an earlier chapter. In the context of this campaign, restoration of the environment, rest for those in poverty, and fair allocation of wealth are the central themes. This means living with environmental limits, ensuring everyone can meet their basic needs, and keeping inequality within reasonable limits.

Such a narrative requires personal change and transformational policies. Christians need to keep a watch on their own use of resources, address poverty directly with our own incomes, speak out against government policies and business practices, and live restorative lives. Transformational policies include a waste free, zero carbon economy and a much fairer tax system. Combating climate change is an essential part of this.

For more information, see the Global campaign http://renewourwor ld.net/, Australia: http://renewourworld.org.au, UK: https://www.tear fund.org/about_you/action/renew_our_world/.

Acting for climate justice

We looked in the last section at advocacy on climate justice. But maybe you want to take things a little further and get involved in direct action. I spoke to pastor and peace activist Jarrod McKenna about this.

'When I'm asked about Christians and non-violent direct action I always think of my friend Simone and the second ever #LoveMakesAWay action in 2014. We professional God-botherers (yep, pastors and priests) were about to be arrested for engaging in a non-violent "sit-in" in a politician's office. Why? Well, our nation was locking up kids. Why? Because these children came to Australia needing safety; that's right, these children were refugees. But I digress from the splendid dagginess of us rabble of reverends and a pack of pastors. There we were on the floor of the politician's office waiting to be arrested in the most polite-hymn-singing-we-baked-brownies-for-the-police-kinda way. Someone mentioned that they had been asked about them breaking the law as a Christian and is 'non-violent direct action' appropriate for Christians. Excitement flashed across the faces of many pastors sitting there. Backs straightened and throats were cleared in preparation to launch into past sermon, papers and quotes to show off our handle of Scripture, Theology and Tradition on the subject on non-violent protest. But all that was all cut short. Before we could start, Simone, a worship leader from a conservative church said,

"Are you talking about the Romans 13 stuff? Um, ok but isn't this written by the same Paul who writes FROM PRISON!?!?!"

Mic drop

Many laughs, and there is was.

The reality that it's ridiculous to quote the Apostle Paul to argue against the witness of his life and the example of our Lord Jesus. Does the Apostle Paul write "submit to the ruling authorities"? You bet. But don't forget: this same Apostle Paul who writes "submit to the authorities" was executed by these authorities because he refused to submit if it meant being unfaithful to Christ! If the authorities ask us to submit and we don't have to compromise faithfulness to Christ's love, we submit. But if submitting means not being faithful to Christ's love, the order is not legitimate.

Then the question becomes, "How are Christians to resist submitting to evil?"

The answer to which is just like Christ did.

Just like the Apostle Paul imitated Christ. (After all, the call to imitate Christ is why we are called Christians). The nonviolent enemy-love of Christ, seen ultimately on the Cross, is the HOW of our lives lived to glorify God. Christ's resurrection is the power in us to love like he has loved us. You don't need to know the Nazi's sought to keep Christians quiet by quoted Romans 13 out of context more than any other passage to know how to interpret Romans 13. We just need to know that Christ is the lens through which we must interpret any passage of Scripture. Then we see this all fits with Romans 12 and the rest of Romans 13 in what the Apostle Paul was calling us to: Calvary-like-love is our model and means of action in the world. Martyrs lives, be they Apostles like Paul, Mark and Peter or people like Polycarp, Perpetua, Felicity, Dirk Williams, Magdalene of Nagasaki, Mariam Vattalil, Depayne Middleton or Martin Luther King Jr., all witness to the call to live Christ's non-violent-love as the model for direct action.'

As another example of what direct action can look like, I spoke to Dr Byron Smith about his experience with direct action against a coal mine.

'In 2014, while working for a church and completing my postgraduate studies in theology, I was arrested while non-violently seeking to block the construction of a hugely destructive coal mine. Twice.

The Whitehaven open cut coal mine at Maules Creek was, at the time, the largest coal mine under construction in Australia. The excavation required the destruction of much of the remaining Leard State Forest; the last stand of White Box gum woodland in the world. It is home to 396 native species, of which at least 34 are threatened. Around a dozen sites sacred to the local Gomeroi/Gamilaray people have been bulldozed, they have been denied access to other sites necessary for ceremony and many of their elders are deeply opposed to the project. Local farmers in one of Australia's most productive agricultural regions are concerned at impacts on the water table. The excavation has already breached the environmental regulations included in its approval. That approval, received in 2013, has long been under a cloud of controversy, with a number of the key figures involved appearing before ICAC in relation to other coal projects. All these issues are well covered by the excellent 2015 independent documentary, *Black Hole*.[39]

And so first in March, then again in June of 2014, I joined with other Christian leaders and ministers in placing my body in the path of machinery required to make the mine operational. On each occasion, our very polite refusal to move from the entrance to the mine site delayed work for many hours. Eventually we were arrested for obstruction.

We were just some of the 350 or so people arrested during the mine's construction, with thousands participating in the blockade in various ways as thirteen groups worked together, representing the largest campaign of civil disobedience against a coal mine in Australia's history. Far from all being 'professional protesters' or 'radical extremists', those arrested included local farmers, doctors and nurses, scientists (including an IPCC author), Christian ministers, lawyers, students, grandparents, a former Australian Rugby captain and a 92 year old WWII Kokoda Trail veteran. All those I met who were involved in the blockade were thoughtful and committed people who had chosen, often at significant personal cost, to stand up for the wellbeing of their neighbours, near and far, human and more than human.

I respect the rule of law and had already pursued many different lawful attempts to defend against these harms. Yet these all failed. As I learned more about the tradition of Christian civil disobedience and the injustices of the mine, it became clear to me that there are times when cherishing God's justice and loving vulnerable neighbours can mean being willing to face the consequences of directly opposing a deeply unjust law. Our non-violent direct action was intended to prevent or delay the deep harms caused by the mine and its deadly product.

Unfortunately, Maules Creek was opened in early 2015 by then Premier Mike Baird, whose administration approved a glut of new and expanded coal mines. In one sense, our efforts were a failure. But the tide of public opinion on coal in Australia has turned, as has the economics of coal worldwide. Every further coal development in this country faces the risk of organised community opposition as their social license evaporates. Furthermore, the Leard Blockade at Maules Creek represented another crucial step in building concrete relationships between three groups with a history of conflict: Aboriginal communities, farmers and environmentalists.

Finally, although this was not my goal in participating, my experiences have sparked countless interesting and often fruitful conversations about the good news of Jesus and its relation to ecological and climate justice.'

Endnotes

1 Graham Readfern, "What does Australian Prime Minister Tony Abbott really think about climate change?" *The Guardian*, 16 June, 2014, accessed 13 February, 2017, https://www.theguardian.com/environment/planet-oz/2014/jun/16/what-does-australian-prime-minister-tony-abbott-really-think-about-climate-change.

2 Karne Barlow, "Climate Institute To Shut Down, But Not Without One Hell Of A Political Parting Shot," *The Huffington Post*, 9 March, 1027, accessed 10 March, 2017, http://www.huffingtonpost.com.au/2017/03/08/climate-institute-will-close-down-but-not-without-one-hell-of-a/.

3 Lisa Cox, "Government rejects gift of solar panels for Kirribilli House," *The Sydney Morning Herald*, 16 March, 2015, accessed 13 February, 2017, http://www.smh.com.au/federal-politics/political-news/government-rejects-gift-of-solar-panels-for-kirribilli-house-20150316-1m0fhl.html.

4 N. T. Wright, *The New Testament and the People of God* (Minneapolis: Fortress Press, 1992) 154.

5 J. S. Richardson, 'Imperium Romanum: Empire and the Language of Power,' *The Journal of Roman Studies*, 81 (1991), 2.

6 J. A. North, "Development of Roman Imperialism," *The Journal of Roman Studies*, 71 (1981): 1-9.

7 Brian J. Walsh and Sylvia C. Keesmaat, *Colossians Remixed: Subverting the Empire* (Downers Grove: Inter-Varsity Press, 2004), 31.

8   Keith Hopkins, "Taxes and Trade in the Roman Empire (200 B.C.-A.D. 400)," *The Journal of Roman Studies*, 70 (1980): 101-125.

9 Wright, *The New Testament and the People of God*, 154. Walsh and Keesmaat, *Colossians Remixed*, 52.

10 Hopkins, *Taxes and Trade*, 101.

11 Hopkins, *Taxes and Trade*, 102.

12 Richard A. Horsley, "The Sicarii: Ancient Jewish "Terrorists"," *The Journal of Religion* 59:4 (1979):435-458.

13   Richard A Horsley, "Josephus and the bandits," *Journal of the study of Judaism* 10:1 (1979): 37-63.

14 Horsley, *Josephus and the bandits*, 45.

15 Aleksandr Solzhenitsyn, *The Gulag Archipelago Volume 1* (New York: Collins, 1974), 168.

16   This idea of Badlands as sacred spaces is developed in Jon Owen, *Muddy Spirituality* (Melbourne: Urban Neighbours of Hope Publications, 2011).

17   Balakrishnan K, Ramaswamy P, Sambandam S, et al., "Air pollution from household solid fuel combustion in India: an overview of exposure and health related information to inform health research priorities," *Global Health Action* 4 (2011), 10.3402/gha.v4i0.5638. doi:10.3402/gha.v4i0.5638.

18   Daniel Gocher, "4 degrees of separation: Santos proves gas not climate solution," *Renew Economy*, 5 May, 2017, accessed 3 June, 2017, http://reneweconomy.com.au/4-degrees-separation-santos-proves-gas-not-climate-solution-87779/.

19   McKenzie Funk, "Did Exxon Lie About Global Warming?" *Rolling Stone*, June 30, 2016, accessed 16 February, 2017, http://www.rollingstone.com/politics/news/did-exxon-lie-about-global-warming-20160630.

20   Yale Climate Connections, "Climate: What did we know and when did we know it?" YouTube video. 7:09 minutes. Published 14 February, 2017. https://www.youtube.com/watch?v=ox5hbkg34Ow&.

21 Funk, *Did Exxon Lie About Global Warming?*

22   Sarah Perkins-Kirkpatrick, Andrew King and Matthew Hale, "Climate change doubled the likelihood of the New South Wales heatwave," *The Conversation*, 16 February, 2017, accessed 16 February, 2017, http://theconversation.com/climate-change-doubled-the-likelihood-of-the-new-south-wales-heatwave-72871?.

23   John Butler, "Scott Morrison Brought A Lump Of Coal And Waved It Around In Parliament," *The Huffington Post*, 9 February, 2017, accessed 13 February, 2017, http://www.huffingtonpost.com.au/2017/02/08/scott-morrison-brought-a-lump-of-coal-and-waved-it-around-in-par/.

24 Dom Vukovic and Penny Evans, "NSW power: Blackouts across the state averted, energy operator says," *ABC News*, 11 February, 2017, accessed 13 February, 2017, http://www.abc.net.au/news/2017-02-10/nsw-power:-blackouts-across-the-state-averted/8260830.

25 Perkins-Kirkpatrick, King and Hale, *Climate change doubled.*

26 Katharine Murphy, "Coalition votes to allow Clean Energy Finance Corporation to invest in carbon capture," *The Guardian*, 30 May, 2017, accessed 3 June, 2017, https://www.theguardian.com/australia-news/2017/may/30/coalition-votes-to-allow-clean-energy-finance-corporation-to-invest-in-carbon-capture.

27 Adam Morton, "'Clean coal' would push up power bills more than wind, solar or gas: analysts," 3 February, 2017, accessed 13 February, 2017, http://www.smh.com.au/federal-politics/political-news/clean-coal-would-push-up-power-bills-more-than-wind-solar-or-gas-analysts-20170203-gu4ow5.html.

28 Christophe McGlade and Paul Ekins, "The geographical distribution of fossil fuels unused when limiting global warming to 2° C," *Nature* 517 (2015): 187-190.

29 Tom DiChristopher, "EPA chief Scott Pruitt says carbon dioxide is not a primary contributor to global warming," *CNBC*, 10 March, 2017, accessed 10 March, 2017, http://www.cnbc.com/2017/03/09/epa-chief-scott-pruitt.html.

30 Coral Davenport, and Eric Lipton, "The Pruitt Emails: E.P.A. Chief Was Arm in Arm With Industry," *The New York Times*, 22 February, 2017, accessed 10 March, 2017, https://www.nytimes.com/2017/02/22/us/politics/scott-pruitt-environmental-protection-agency.html?_r=0.

31 BBC News, "Oxfam says wealth of richest 1% equal to other 99%," *BBC News*, 18 January, 2016, accessed 10 March, 2017, http://www.bbc.com/news/business-35339475.

32 Larry Elliot, "World's eight richest people have same wealth as poorest 50%," *The Guardian*, 16 January, 2017, accessed 3 June, 2017, https://www.theguardian.com/global-development/2017/jan/16/worlds-eight-richest-people-have-same-wealth-as-poorest-50.

33 John W. Welch, "Legal and social perspectives on Robbers in First-century Judea," *BYU Studies Quarterly* 36:3 (1996): 141-153.

34 Joel B Brinkley, "U.S. vs Microsoft: The overview; U.S judge says Microsoft violated antitrust laws with predatory behaviour," *The New York Times*, 4 April, 2000, accessed 17 June, 2017, http://www.nytimes.com/2000/04/04/business/us-vs-microsoft-overview-us-judge-says-microsoft-violated-antitrust-laws-with.html.

35 TEAR Fund, "UK Christians join global push to press and pray for action on climate change," *TEAR Fund*, 23 February, 2017, accessed 5 April, 2017, http://www.tearfund.org/en/media/press_releases/uk_christians_join_global_push_to_press_and_pray_for_action_on_climate_change/.

36 Nives Dolsak, and Aseem Prakash, "Are we overreacting to US withdrawal from the Paris Agreement on climate?," *The Conversation*, 2 June, 2017, accessed 17 June, 2017, https://theconversation.com/are-we-overreacting-to-us-withdrawal-from-the-paris-agreement-on-climate-78741.

37 Alex Evans, and Richard Gower, "The restorative economy: Completing our unfinished Millennium Jubilee," *Tearfund*, 2015, accessed 5 April, 2017, http://renewourworld.net/wp-content/uploads/2017/01/Restorative-Economy-Summary-Report-Tearfund.pdf.

38 Evans and Gower, *The restorative economy*.

39 Joao Dujon Pereira, *Black Hole*. DVD. Directed by Joao Dujon Pereira, Melbourne: Optical Alkemi, 2015.

AFTERWORD

I guess I could have finished this short book with the chapter on climate action, it would have been a good place to end. But I can't help myself, and a short summing up is in order. What I set out to do was really quite simple. Firstly, I wanted to remind readers that justice an intrinsic part of God's nature, an expression of divine love. Secondly, to love God means also to love our neighbour, which is to show justice towards them. If all you have is right doctrine (orthodoxy) without right practice (orthopraxy) then I'm afraid you fall foul of James' principle of faith without works being dead. This means restoring them to their rights, as being made in the image of God, is at the heart of how the Hebrew word *mishpat* is often used.

Thirdly, if we love justice, we must deal with climate change. Climate change affects all of the justice issues we have examined: poverty, slavery, refugees and Indigenous rights. Indeed, climate change affects anything we might consider a justice issue; all of the Sustainable Development Goals. Care about people, and we have to care about the climate. Want to restore the rights of people? We need to deal with the climate. That means understanding the role we play, and the power we have to determine the future of the climate. Such power involves us taking actions, from something as simple as signing a petition, to our vote, to how we might disrupt a system that produces injustice. This means living truly just or righteous lives.

But I want to finish with one more challenge. Pope Francis has set the tone for his papacy early on by his encyclical, Laudato Si'. Francis takes the relationship between the economy and ecology seriously. We could have anticipated this given that the name he took is taken from St Francis of Assisi, the man who reputedly preached a sermon to the birds. His Canticle of Brother Sun and Sister Moon recognises a kinship beyond the human. In particular, he writes

> Praised be You my Lord through our Sister, Mother Earth who sustains and governs us, producing varied fruits with coloured flowers and herbs.

For some, this will be a stretch. Language of Mother Earth might smack of earth religion, but recall Paul writes of the Earth groaning in birth pains (Romans 8:19-23), and Isaiah proclaims that the trees of the field clap their hands (Isaiah 55:12). Scripture has a long tradition of personifying the rest of creation as agents of praise to God and witnesses to our sin against it and God.

Can we embrace the non-human as our neighbour as well, as an object of our love? You needn't think this way to care about climate change, we know the impacts that are happening now, and the possible impacts in the future if we do nothing. And yet can we go further? We know that humans are made in the image and likeness of God, and so to love God means we must love our neighbour. But what if loving God means also treasuring what he has made and takes delight in (Psalm 104:24-25, 31)? What if our fates are so intertwined that the resurrection of the dead means redemption for creation as well (Romans 8:19-23)? We can spend so much time drawing a line between humans and non-humans, that we forget that there is only one line to be drawn, between creator and creatures. We might be more valuable to God than sparrows, but sparrows are also valuable to God (Matthew 10:28-31).

African-American author and poet Alice Walker says that 'Activism is my rent for living on the planet.' Let me finish this all too brief treatment of the interaction between climate change and justice with the suggestion that 'Activism is our way of mirroring God's love of justice, righteousness and steadfast love, and how we love our neighbours, present and future, in a warming world.'

www.ingramcontent.com/pod-product-compliance
Lightning Source LLC
LaVergne TN
LVHW051349080426
835509LV00020BA/3360